Other books by Richard G. Geldard

Emerson and Universal Mind
Emerson and the Dream of America
Anaxagoras and Universal Mind
Pythagoras and the Way of Truth
The Essential Transcendentalists
The Spiritual Teachings of Ralph Waldo Emerson
Remembering Heraclitus
God in Concord
The Traveler's Key to Ancient Greece
The Find at Ephesus, a novel
The Vision of Emerson

The Soul's Journey

The Soul's Journey

A History of Human Being

Richard G. Geldard PhD

Copyright © 2016 Richard G. Geldard PhD
All rights reserved.
ISBN-13: 9781530047888
ISBN-10: 1530047889
Library of Congress Control Number: 2016903321
CreateSpace Independent Publishing Platform
North Charleston, South Carolina

Your book has been assigned a CreateSpace ISBN.

Member ID 507043

For Seven Good Friends

Contents

Introduction · xi

Chapter 1 The Problems and Challenges · · · · · · · · · · · · · · · · · 1
Chapter 2 Pre-history, The Rig Veda and Vedanta · · · · · · · · · 16
Chapter 3 Egypt and Reincarnation · · · · · · · · · · · · · · · · · · 33
Chapter 4 Greece and the Psyche · · · · · · · · · · · · · · · · · · · 45
Chapter 5 Christianity and the Soul · · · · · · · · · · · · · · · · · 61
Chapter 6 Neoplatonism and Christianity · · · · · · · · · · · · · · 75
Chapter 7 Hermes Elevates the Soul · · · · · · · · · · · · · · · · · 89
Chapter 8 Ficino and the Soul In Florence · · · · · · · · · · · · · 107
Chapter 9 Emerson and the Over- Soul · · · · · · · · · · · · · · · 121
Chapter 10 Consciousness and Soul in our Time · · · · · · · · · · 136

Introduction

To BEGIN A study of something as ephemeral as the soul is either a fool's errand or an arrogant enterprise doomed to failure. Somewhere between these extremes, however, keeping foolishness at bay and being aware of the sin of arrogance may still serve a useful purpose. In this regard, I have elected to commence this exploration with both warning and encouragement from one of my most trusted teachers: the preeminent Vedantist philosopher, Sri Aurobindo, whose monumental writings have been my personal companions for some years. In addition, he was particularly important for this effort because he was a man from two worlds: both West and East. Educated in England, he moved to India during the British colonial period and lived to witness Indian independence, the establishment of which took place to honor him on his birthday, so crucial was his role in breaking the hold of British rule and in helping to found the world's most populous democracy.

Among his many books is The *Supramental Manifestation* and in it is the first chapter entitled "The Reincarnating Soul" part of a much longer piece entitled *The Problem of Rebirth*. Here is its first paragraph, both as warning and encouragement:

> *Our mind is a sleepy or careless sentry and allows anything to pass the gates which seems to it decently garbed or wears a*

Introduction

plausible appearance or can mumble anything that resembles some familiar password. Especially is this so in subtle matters, those remote from the concrete facts of our physical life and environment. Even men who will reason carefully and acutely in ordinary matters and there consider vigilance against error an intellectual or a practical duty, are yet content with the most careless stumbling when they get upon higher and more difficult ground. Where precision and subtle thinking are most needed, there they are most impatient of it and averse to the labour demanded of them. Men can manage fine thought about palpable things, but to think subtly about the subtle is too great a strain on the grossness of our intellects; so we are content with making a dab at the truth, like the painter who threw his brush at his picture when he could not get the effect that he desired. We mistake the smudge that results for the perfect form of a verity.

The task, then, that Sri Aurobindo undertakes in the 170 pages of *The Problem of Rebirth* assigns to anyone either foolish or arrogant enough to undertake the project, is to avoid trying to paint a definitive painting of the soul or to erupt in frustration by throwing his brush at the canvas and calling the smudge the truth. Rather, the task to be undertaken is to examine some of the cultural and spiritual efforts to understand the nature of the soul and to place the result in the context of human life and death.

The challenge for a task of this subtle nature is that in our recent culture, aside from a variety of religious doctrines holding fast to traditional definitions, we encounter the absence of soul from sight. Books like William Barrett's *The Death of the Soul* (1986) is an example of this decline in philosophy and culture in general and its replacement by our intense interest in the nature of consciousness. This shift effectively removes an expansive vision of human existence beyond our present lives into the vagaries of a consciousness centered in the brain or mind. As the back cover description of Barrett's book has it, Barrett "enables us to see how philosophical thought has taken us to where we stand, and why questions of the soul figure so faintly in the minds of today's technocratic intellectuals." Today, of course, we are known as "device people," but that is another story.

Consciousness studies by themselves are presently centered mainly in the laboratories of neuroscience, where cell biology and electrical circuitry rule exploratory investigation. In a more esoteric setting, however, consciousness studies in the wisdom traditions (our focus in this exploration) must perforce include study of the soul if for no other reason than to reaffirm the traditional presence of such an entity in human life and nature. If consciousness and soul are taken together, human nature then possesses a fullness of articulation that recognizes the rich experiences of many lives. As Emerson put it, a spiritual experience is its own proof. No microscope or ultrasound can measure it.

The soul, then, may be unfathomable, but it exists in the records of cultures of nearly every period, language, belief and experience. According to some sages and traditions, the soul may be dormant or illusory, and it may awaken and be felt or imagined, return asleep or remain active, but such an important entity warrants attention. Barrett says to conclude his book,

What shall it profit a whole civilization, or culture, if it gains knowledge and power over the material world, but loses any

Introduction

adequate idea of the conscious mind, the human self, at the center of all that power? It would have been more powerful had he added soul.

Barrett echoes the warning in Mark 8:38. What profit indeed? The loss of soul to power will destroy the Earth as surly as if a meteor or all-out nuclear war would. And without soul the latter is more likely to happen.

As will become evident in the material to follow, the major influences in the understanding we have inherited about the soul, whether acknowledged or not, come from the central chapters of this text, numbers five and six, the Greek and Early Christian periods. The material on both sides, however, provide background in one case and the evolution of soul in the other.

How we respond to the challenge to consider the vitality represented by the existence of the soul in human nature and its history may have consequences for the future. This book is an effort to re-awaken the concept of soul as an active attribute of human intellect and consciousness. I would add that this book is also a publication taken from a series of lectures given at the University of Philosophical Research and has been enriched by the responses I received. We so-called moderns have become so disconnected from the animated and feeling part of the life of the mind, that opening up the subject of a soul at the core of our living, breathing selves can have a dramatic effect on how we perceive, not only our daily lives, but also about how we think about ultimate meaning of the days we have been given.

CHAPTER 1

The Problems and Challenges

To BEGIN, HERE are the problems and with them, the challenges. How do we approach the topic of knowledge of the soul when we understand at the outset that the knowledge we desire is destined to be uncertain and seemingly based on opinion. I say 'seemingly' to suggest that perhaps we can do and say more than opinionate. The rational and gifted Greeks divided knowledge into opinion, *doxa*, and truth, *aletheia*. In the latter case, their sense of what was ultimately true was based not only on experience but also on what was remembered.[1]

If we approach the subject as a problem of remembering the nature of the soul, we then have to choose among the variety of human disciplines which one will be most revealing and effective. We might normally say that the subject of the soul is a religious or theological topic, leading us then to a study of world religions and the writings of theologians. Or, we might look to science as the empirical study of what is real and demonstrably true on the subject. We might explore the works of mythology and symbolism as representations of the soul in a variety of traditions, searching in the process for signs of convergence suggestive of an accurate

---

1 The Greek word *aletheia* breaks down into a word meaning not forgetting, or remembering, suggesting that truth is something remembered and that philosophy was the business of remembering what is true.

picture. We might also choose philosophy and its subset metaphysics as a rational examination of soul in the context of consciousness studies, again in various traditions and historic eras.

These choices all have limitations and advantages, particularly if we choose to remain within a particular discipline. In the latter case, if we choose philosophy, we encounter the bias of the academy, the traditional and limiting role of the university in exploring any topic of uncertain and questionable reality. The obvious conclusion is that any approach to the subject of the soul must be cross-cultural and interdisciplinary. This approach means that we need to include and respect the philosophers of the Indus river basin, the priests of ancient Egypt, the natural philosophers of Early Greece, the Hermetists and Early Church fathers, the revolutionaries of the Italian Renaissance, the Transcendentalists, as well as the psychologists of our own era who posit the role of spirit in human nature as crucial to human existence and destiny.

The challenges that confront us are linguistic and experiential. The early history of what is now India is expressed in Sanskrit, the proto-language of Indo-European languages. As we shall explore, a word like Purusha, for example, contains in its roots and meaning one of the earliest references to soul. In the hieroglyphs of early Egypt there appear multiple notions of soul, particularly in words like Ba and Ka. Not only are the terms problematic in themselves, the translations into other languages and traditions throughout history create challenges of meaning, which in the case of soul have implications including issues of immortality and transcendence.

A major challenge arises when we explore mystical and spiritual traditions in their historical context and in their adaptations throughout their longevity. An example is the notion of soul in the Italian Renaissance in which ancient Roman and Greek concepts of soul confront the doctrines of the Roman Papacy with its confining Inquisition. Martyrs like Giordano Bruno paid the price for his inherence to the nature and destiny of soul taken from Roman, Greek and Hermetic interpretations. Quite literally, our life hangs in the balance.

Later, the Eighteenth Century European Enlightenment, with its freedom of philosophic exploration and scientific discoveries, thinkers either ignored the topic of soul or changed its meaning to include feeling and inner conviction. To complicate matters, the study of consciousness entered the scene in the ensuing works of thinkers like Descartes, Kant and, later, Hegel. During this time, even the definition of soul suffered alteration, essentially from the source of immortality to the human center of feeling. Soul was also redefined as the source of conscience, the arbiter of good and evil.

With Romanticism, soul recaptured its spiritual nature in part but also assumed a role as a higher feeling, an essential characteristic of the noble warmth of feeling. Complicating matters came the notion of soul-mate, the connection between two human beings destined for a lifetime of being together in harmony and completion. Indeed, the idea of completion became the highest form of soul connection, as if two people came together in recognition of a destined relationship, perhaps even going back many lifetimes.

As we shall explore further, the early Romantic sensibility as formed and expressed by Coleridge and Wordsworth in particular, crossed the Atlantic and was transformed into New England Transcendentalism by Ralph Waldo Emerson, Henry Thoreau and the Concord Circle. In Emerson's work the soul returned to its original power as the eternal essence within human nature and even into Nature itself. Although the influence of this movement suffered in the devastation of the American Civil War, essential elements of it carried forward and combined with subsequent religious and spiritual movements in America.

This fertile ground at the beginning of the Twentieth Century attracted Eastern thinking in the presence of spiritual leaders of Vedanta and Buddhism taught by figures such as Vivekananda, Krishnamurti and Sri Aurobindo. The result of Eastern transmission of these doctrines into the West influenced the interest in the soul and began to influence Christian teachings as well.

This influence had its peak in the turbulent Sixties and Seventies in the New Age, spawning a culture of mystical and visionary movements in which the soul was revived once again in ordinary thinking and in books like Thomas Moore's *Care of the Soul* and *Soul Mates*, among other titles. Meanwhile, this counter culture was attacked by critics in the materialistic mode whose intellectual cynicism finally drove the New Age underground by the close of the Twentieth Century.

As a result, the soul retreated into the human psyche as an ill-defined and troublesome entity if it survived at all. A quotation from Moore may illustrate the way in which psychology has explored the idea of the soul:

> *It is impossible to define precisely what the soul is. Definition is an intellectual enterprise anyway: the soul prefers to imagine. We know intuitively that soul has to do with genuineness and depth, as when we say certain music has soul or a remarkable person is soulful. When you look closely at the image of soulfulness, you see that it is tied to life in all its particulars—good*

food, satisfying conversation, genuine friends, and experiences that stay in the memory and touch the heart. Soul is revealed in attachment, love, and community, as well as in retreat on behalf of inner communing and intimacy. (Care of the Soul, xi-xii)

It is clear in this example how the term 'soul' is imagined by secular writers rather than theologians or religious apologists. If we accept Moore's description of the reductive soul, we might just as well leave the word alone and examine some more accessible spiritual term. But as we will discover, Hillman treats the subject of soul in much greater depth. The passage above, however, illustrates the way the word is treated and understood by a great majority of modern readers and thinkers.

An example of this greater depth from Hillman comes from the beginning of his book entitled *The Soul's Code*. His first mention of the word 'soul' comes not from his own sense of it but rather from Plato's *Republic*. We are sympathetic with this slight of hand because it conforms with our own sense of how to approach this study. Here is how this introduction is presented:

The soul of each of us is given a unique daimon before we are born, and it has selected an image or pattern that we live on earth. This soul-companion, the daimon, guides us here; in the process of arrival, however, we forget all that took place and believe we come empty into this world. The daimon remembers what is in your image and belongs to your pattern, and therefore your daimon is the carrier of your destiny. As explained by the greatest of later Platonists, Plotinus (A.D. 205– 270), we elected the body, the parents, the place, and the circumstances that suited the soul and that, as the myth says, belong to its necessity. This suggests that the circumstances, including my body and my parents whom I may curse, are my soul's own choice— and I do not understand this because I have forgotten.[2]

The Greek word *daimon* closely corresponds to "in-dwelling spirit." The idea of the daimon as a pattern or template for our life frees the soul somewhat from that characteristic, but only somewhat. Plato's soul is unique to the individual and is part of the body/mind/soul structure. In fact, Plato's soul has its own body, mind and spirit or daimon in its journey in an embodiment. We shall have more to say about Hillman's soul in later chapters.

Another crucial figure in the modern world of psychology is C.G. Jung, whose explorations into the world of soul continues to attract serious seekers into its nature and meaning. Jung saw the soul as the heart of psychological experience as defined by our world of imagination, feeling and consciousness. It does not extend to eternity, at least not in Jung' formal writing. The recent revelations in the long-hidden *Red Book*, however, reveal a more private and expanded vision.

This kind of secretive, private knowledge of the soul in writing such as Jung's takes place following sweeping shifts in attitudes and beliefs like the Enlightenment, which swept away seemingly outmoded explanations of the human instrument and its attributes. As we shall see, even the theories of where the soul was situated in the body changed from era to era. Jean Gebser in his monumental *Ever-Present Origin* actually graphed the changes where the soul was located.

---

[2] *Hillman, James (2013-02-06). The Soul's Code: In Search of Character and Calling* (Kindle Locations 161-167). Random House Publishing Group. Kindle Edition.

According to Gebser, in the Archaic Period the soul was universal, that is it existed throughout the universe, and human beings were within its powers and breathed its essence. In his Magical Period the soul was found in blood and semen, the life-giving power creating and sustaining life itself. In the Mythical Period it rested in the diaphragm and heart, symptomatic of breath and life. In the Mental Period, the soul could be found and experienced in the spinal cord and the brain. This interpretation exists today, although it is not widely held. Finally, in the Integral Period, projecting forward, the rejection of the duality of body and mind in Descartes, the soul rests in the cerebral cortex and in the humoral or fluids.

What is important about these shifts in belief and interpretation is that where the soul is thought to be found with the human structure not only shifts in the climate of opinion, but it also reflects development in scientific understanding, particularly in biology. In the Eastern traditions, the soul has long belonged in the center of the heart as a flame. It is more typical in the West for it to move about in religious doctrine, linguistic usage and scientific progress. That the soul is believed not to exist at all has also been a consistent opinion on the part of materialists and atheists.

It is important to add here that Gebser's description of the location of a soul in the human instrument does not make any reference to cultural tradition. As such, it does not make a distinction between the broad traditions of East and West, those divisions with which we are the most familiar. Here, I return to Jung for a while to look at the complications involved with definitions of soul, mind, and psyche. The following paragraph is from a lecture given by Dr. Jung on the topic of "The Tibetan Book of the Great Liberation."

The Problems and Challenges

DR. EVANS-WENTZ has entrusted me with the task of commenting on a text which contains an important exposition of Eastern 'psychology'. The very fact that I have to use inverted commas shows the dubious applicability of this term. It is perhaps not superfluous to mention that the East has produced nothing equivalent to what we call psychology, but rather philosophy or metaphysics. Critical philosophy, the mother of modern psychology, is as foreign to the East as to medieval Europe. Thus the word 'mind', as used in the East, has the connotation of something metaphysical. Our Western conception of mind has lost this connotation since the Middle Ages, and the word has now come to signify a 'psychic function'. Despite the fact that we neither know nor pretend to know what psyche' is, we can deal with the phenomenon of mind'. We do not assume that the mind is a metaphysical entity or that there is any connexion between an individual mind and a hypothetical Universal Mind. Our psychology is, therefore, a science of mere phenomena without any metaphysical implications. The development of Western philosophy during the last two centuries has succeeded in isolating the mind in its own sphere and in severing it from its primordial oneness with the universe. Man himself has ceased to be the microcosm and eidolon of the cosmos, and his 'anima' is no longer the consubstantial scintilla, or spark of the Anima Mundi, the World Soul....Western psychology knows the mind as the mental functioning of a psyche. It is the 'mentality' of an individual. An impersonal Universal Mind is still to be met with in the sphere of philosophy, where it seems to be a relic of the original human 'soul'. This picture of our Western outlook may seem a little drastic, but I do not think it is far from the truth.

This excerpt contains important insights into the problems and challenges of knowing the soul. First, Jung reminds us that Eastern

The Soul's Journey

traditions do not recognize the Western traditions of "Critical Philosophy." Eastern philosophy is primarily metaphysics, that is the rational and intuitive examination of the reality of Being. Then, Jung makes the statement that the Western concept of mind, unlike the Eastern view, disappeared in the Middle Ages, never to reappear. It was later in his career that Jung began to entertain a more metaphysical view of mind through the extraordinary mind of Wolfgang Pauli, the quantum physicist with whom Jung worked as a therapist. The Eastern mind did indeed reappear in the West.

It is through the work of physicists like Pauli that the study of consciousness in the West began to reach into the realm of Eastern metaphysics and to connect the human mind to Universal Mind. Next, Jung dismisses the traditional role of the soul in human relationship to the cosmos, giving the mind through consciousness that role.

In the final segment, we see Jung's role as therapist emerge in his primary concern with the mind as psyche. Inasmuch as he also indicates the presence of spirit, although inadvertently, we are left in Jung an incomplete picture of the complete attributes of the human being. What shall we do then to proceed with our investigation? How are we to see ourselves in existence? What are our connected facets of being? We know we have a body, a physical biome of matter, energy, solid and liquid, and chemical in great measure. We have a mind of great expanse and function, capable of minute detail and control, as well as the ability to comprehend the laws of nature. This mind of ours possesses a variety, or better yet, a continuum of consciousness from coma to enlightenment and every state in between. And if we are not enamored with materialism, we may also possess spirit or soul, attributes not the same as consciousness, mind or body in its nature nor purpose.

The Problems and Challenges

How then do we proceed to explore this latter possibility? We can search the world's literature, its philosophy, and its religious history and doctrines. We can examine the personal experiences of individuals, their moments of illumination and conviction, the testimonies of the saints and so-called madmen. We can catalogue the accounts of those who remember past lives as evidence of reincarnation and even report such memories of our own and those near us.

What has been left out of this range of approaches are the assertions of "proofs" offered by psychics and the experts of parapsychology and other mystical explorers. And why will I neglect them? This is not an easy question to answer, because when we have personal experiences and have come close to perceptions we might call mystical, our sympathies are aroused and we feel anxious to share them. But we hesitate, thinking that perhaps something more definitive, more empirical will arise as proof.

However, there are sensible reasons to hesitate. There are lessons in this matter, the first and foremost from Jesus in the wilderness, a place we have all been and been approached by the tempter, but Jesus said, "You must not put the Lord your God to the test."[3] And if this advice is not attractive, consider a more practical example closer to home. Ralph Waldo Emerson had a spiritual experience as a young man walking across Boston Common at twilight. He recorded the experience in his journal and then included it in *Nature*, his first published work.

Here is what he wrote;

Crossing a bare common, in snow puddles, at twilight, under a clouded sky, without having in my thoughts any occurrence of

---
[3] Matthew 4:7

special good fortune, I have enjoyed a perfect exhilaration. I am glad to the brink of fear...Standing on the bare ground, — my head bathed by the blithe air, and uplifted into infinite space, — all mean egotism vanishes. I become a transparent eye-ball; I am nothing; I see all; the currents of the Universal Being circulate through me; I am part or particle of God.

When the book was published, this revelation – because it was one – prompted some public ridicule and some even thought Emerson insane. The criticism did not deter him, of course, in publishing his essays and giving his lectures on Idealism, but he was cautious in revealing similar experiences. Then, later in his career he published an essay entitled "Demonology," in which he made a clear distinction between what he termed intuitive personal revelations and the kind of spiritualism which was widely practiced in the Nineteenth and Early Twentieth Centuries, particularly in America and England.

He basically argued that such conversations with the dead, ghostly appearances and tricks of the parlor, as he called them, gave true spiritual experiences a bad name. He put the matter this way:

And I find nothing in fables more astonishing than my experience in every hour. One moment of a man's life is a fact so stupendous as to take the lustre out of all fiction. The lovers of marvels, of what we call the occult and unproved sciences, of mesmerism, of astrology, of coincidences, of intercourse by writing or by rapping or by painting, with departed spirits, need not reproach us with incredulity because we are slow to accept their statement. It is not the incredibility of the fact, but a certain want of harmony between the action and the agents. We are used to vaster wonders than these that are alleged. In the hands of poets, of devout and simple minds, nothing in the line of their character and genius would surprise us. But we should look for the style of the great artist in it, look for completeness and harmony. Nature never works like a conjuror, to surprise, rarely by shocks, but by infinite graduation; so that we live embosomed in sounds we do not hear, scents we do not smell, spectacles we see not, and by innumerable impressions so softly laid on that though important we do not discover them until our attention is called to them.

For Spiritism, it shows that no man, almost, is fit to give evidence. Then I say to the amiable and sincere among them, these matters are quite too important than that I can rest them on any legends. If I have no facts, as you allege, I can very well wait for them. I am content and occupied with such miracles as I know, such as my eyes and ears daily show me, such as humanity and astronomy. If any others are important to me they will certainly be shown to me.

In effect, the cosmos, nature and human existence is miracle enough for us if we pay attention. All the advances of science have not offered empirical proof of how this universe came into being and what will be its destiny. The sense-based materialists will keep trying to explain, but the key is that mystery will prevail, and the unknown will survive all of our digging and explanations. Here is Emerson's final warning about intruding upon the sacred mysteries of existence:

Before we acquire great power we must acquire wisdom to use it well. Animal magnetism inspires the prudent and moral with a certain terror; so the divination of contingent events, and the alleged second-sight of the pseudo-spiritualists. There are many things of which a wise man might wish to be ignorant, and these are such. Shun them as you would the secrets of the undertaker and the butcher. The best are never demoniacal or magnetic; leave this limbo to the Prince of the power of the air. The lowest angel is better. It is the height of the animal; below the region of the divine. Power as such is not known to the angels.

If you thought, as I did, of the immense dangers unleashed by nuclear power and as yet undeveloped weapons, you are on the right page of this inquiry. Clearly genuine spiritual power is not for the ignorant or destructively inclined. We have enough trouble with firearms not to unleash the kinds of powers that tempted Jesus in the desert of his temptations.

How then shall this inquiry proceed? At first we shall look at the earliest historical records where the soul is imagined and included in human experience. These texts all suffer from the errors of translation, especially where those doing the translating were wedded to later learning and inevitable bias. This kind of error was typical of the scholarship of the Nineteenth Century where the inquiry into ancient records was not treated with adequate respect and translators felt they were correcting the record rather than reporting knowledge. Errors of this kind appeared in both form and content. For example, translation of ancient Greek poetry and drama often appeared in iambic pentameter, the form followed by Shakespeare, rather than in the forms followed by the ancient poets. Later in the Twentieth Century these errors were corrected, and as a result, meaning changed as well.

We will try to reference only the latest research except where we find a translator who understands the spiritual intent and significance of an text and accords it what the writer intended to express. An example of this kind of reference are the translations of Thomas Taylor, whose 1803 publication of Plato's *Works* reflects the spirit of the dialogues which later efforts did not. Taylor treats the soul in ways that later more secular texts exclude.

Also, it is relevant that we look at the notion of "a history of soul." History, as such, is usually a temporal account of events and is commonly the accounts of those who exercise power, hence accounts of wars, conquest, economics, scientific progress, and politics. A history of the soul begins loosely with Gebser's division of periods (see above). In *The Ever-Present Origin*, Chapter Six is entitled "On the History of the Phenomena of Soul and Spirit." Gebser's overall aim is to explore the nature of consciousness, and Chapter Six explores that theme in relation to soul and thought, the soul being essentially interior and thought more spacial.

Gebser begins this chapter with a warning to himself not to approach soul, spirit and consciousness with an excessive rationality, an error made in Greek history by the followers of Aristotle, who took his disagreements with his teacher Plato as a sign to reject the master completely. The result was an early strain of materialism, which in the case of science grew stronger until its final victory in the Enlightenment and dominance in the concrete halls of academe today.

What took place in the Hellenic period following Plato and Aristotle is that the birth of consciousness that began among the Pre-Socratics, opened up the study of thought itself as a history of the conflict between ignorance and knowledge, whereas in the past that view or vision of consciousness did not exist. As the philosopher

Eric Voegelin put it, this was "the event in which the process of reality becomes luminous to itself. It is not an information received, but an insight arising from the dialogue of the soul..."[4]

The phrase "becomes luminous to itself" deserves serious attention. When a level of consciousness becomes evident to an individual in what Socrates called the examined life, the mind becomes luminous to itself as an event of self-awareness. An interior observer emerges, not evident before, and takes note of the change in the conscious mind, which in turn becomes luminous to itself. So too, I will argue, with the soul, which when it becomes an object of conscious inquiry also may become luminous to itself. These events can be traced in a history and can be discovered and recorded to form part of the history of the soul.

We have been able to describe with some accuracy the birth of consciousness and also to describe the history of the birth of a philosophy of consciousness in early Greek thought, but the same effort has not been made with the soul, whose history is tied closely to cultural myth and religious belief and doctrine. It is simple enough to trace that history, but what is more challenging, and the central aim of this effort, is to see if it is possible to make the soul "luminous to itself" by affirming that the soul is a single entity in its essence and reality and has been described through time in a variety of ways more reflective of context than in isolation.

In this effort, no definition of the nature of the soul will precede the effort to describe its history. To do so would be to fit Cinderella's slipper to the correct foot as if the seeking Prince knew her address. The truth is that he forgot her face and must travel the kingdom to find his soul mate. In other words, we cannot know the landscape of our destination until we actually arrive.

---

[4] Eric Voegelin, *The Ecumenic Age*, Louisiana State University press, 1974, p.186

CHAPTER 2

Pre-history, The Rig Veda and Vedanta

THE SEARCH FOR the soul begins as an archeological enterprise, which is to say that like archeologists we must uncover the foundation stones of what came to be the temples dedicated to the story of a sacred human artifact. When we think of artifacts we think first of tools, objects found in caves and sites of habitation indicative of human development. Also around 40,000 years ago, we begin to find cave art, beautiful drawings of animals signed by human hands from sites all over the world: South Africa, Australia, India, Europe, and North and South America.

Our fascination with cave art stems mostly from the realization that even at this early period in human development, we augmented our daily lives with artistic creation denoting some deep spiritual longing and purpose. Scholars from nearly every culture have suggested that the impulse to enter these deep and forbidding caves, some nearly impossible to penetrate, represent places of worship, the domain of shamans who were the priests of their cultures, and that the paintings reveal an advance in consciousness and a concern for the afterlife.

In addition to cave art, whatever its meaning or intent, are examples of sculpture, such as the so-called Venus of Willandorf, a female figure found in 1908 in Austria and thought to represent a fertility symbol or Earth Mother goddess. The figure is dated at 26,000 to 28,000 years old, and like the cave paintings, a time of magical thinking. Added to these artifacts, we now have the recent discovery at Gobekli Tepe in Turkey, a major excavation of symbolic and possibly religious importance dated at 12,000 years ago.

At Gobekli over 200 huge stone pillars formed in circles are carved with animals, again suggesting magical and mythic symbolism. To what purpose the site was built is to this date unknown, but further excavation may reveal why this rare and mysterious site was constructed and then carefully covered up so as to preserve it. But the point for our excavation is that even here we do not find evidence of the soul in human expression except in the clear sense of a sacred purpose.

Even if we move ahead 10,000 years to the Archaic Period, we learn from Gebser that the soul has yet to make an appearance. He explains the period by saying of it, "It is akin, if not identical, to the original state of biblical paradise: a time where the soul is yet dormant, a time of complete non-differentiation of man and the universe."[5]

The crucial implication here, but not stated by Gebser, is that when we do find references to the soul it indicates a loss of innocence, a conscious awareness of loss of unity with divinity. It is, to connect the symbolism to the Garden of Eden, that although Adam and Eve are ejected from paradise on Earth, God grants them a remnant, a key to paradise if we are capable of finding the door, or gate to return to paradise. As we shall see, this idea of soul as a remnant is found in many cultural myths. Through error or disobedience or merely the jealousy of the gods, a human being

---
5 Gebser, p. 43

is torn apart, his body scattered through the world, left only with a remnant or soul as a sign of redemption. The classic examples are Osiris and Dionysus.

The symbolism is clear enough. In order to be "reassembled' in a full human form as the gods, or God, created, the message is that we must awaken the soul to its essential task, which is re-union, to be reunited with divinity, a separation which was perhaps unintended. The mystery of course, is why humanity was created in the first place with the possibility of disobedience as part of its nature. Why, we ask of the writers of Genesis, was the commandment given not to eat of the fruit of the tree, the symbol of the knowledge of good and evil, located as it is in the geometrically focused center of the garden? But the answer to that mystery forms the long and complex tale of religious belief and doctrine. It is a mystery that philosophy too has undertaken to resolve, without success. It may even be one reason why at the end of the Renaissance, philosophy tore itself away from religion in its effort to explore the truth of reality on and in its own terms.

To return, however, to the above quote from Gebser, he concludes his comment about the dormant soul with the reason for the dormancy, that it was "a time of complete non-differentiation of man and the universe." First, we note the use of the term 'dormant.' The soul was present in the human framework but was inactive. To be dormant is like the seed in the ground before it comes to life. It is not like consciousness, which has its degrees of activity from coma to enlightened self-awareness. A dormant soul, on the other hand, suggests inactivity, and the reason for it, Gebser suggests, has to do with non-differentiation, or better yet, unity, a oneness with the universe in which the individual soul was not needed.

If that image, or symbolism, has relevance to the task at hand – the task of knowing the soul – then we can speculate that the activity or rousing to life of the soul stems from a loss of unity with the universe, a case of radical separation. If so, we ask, what was the reason for this separation? One answer, given credence by the texts we have at our disposal from the Pre-Socratics, The Vedas, and the Tao Te Ching, is that human beings either fell from grace or became self-conscious individuals, no longer integrated seamlessly into nature, family, tribe, and community. This loss, formulated by the Church Fathers as the Fall of Man, became the ruling principle of salvation doctrine.

At any rate, whatever the cause, the soul awakens and begins to take an active role in human life and destiny in the effort to reconnect human beings to the universe, to paradise in the garden, which only later becomes heaven, a term which does not even enter the English language as a divine realm until the Sixteenth Century in England.

But we are getting ahead of our investigation. We have other cultures and histories to explore. From the point of view of chronology, it is uncertain whether it would be accurate to begin in the East or in Egypt, but the depth of resources leans us towards the Indic sources first, and the document of record is the Rig Veda, where we find, "Adoration to the Ancient Seers, The First Path Makers."

Eastern References to Soul

1. The Rig Veda
My own source of choice for a study of the Rig Veda comes from a text of four translations of the Sanskrit assembled by Dr. Jean Le

Pre-history, The Rig Veda and Vedanta

Meé, whom I have known as a friend for more than thirty years. His Rig Veda was published in a limited edition of 100 copies by the Jain Publishing Company in 2004. The edition I am using is number ninety-eight, and I have also had some direct input from Dr. Le Meé, which I will document as we proceed.

As Le Meé has noted in his useful introduction, the task of translating the Sanskrit of the Rig Veda into any language is extremely difficult. In fact the great scholar Sri Aurobindo said that the task was virtually impossible. It should also be noted that the English translation included in this text was first published in 1975 by Alfred Knopf. Even with the problems of translation, we proceed in this study not to interpret the Sanskrit text, but rather to find references to references to the soul in Indic belief and practice.

Le Meé is intent on explaining to the general reader and non-Sanskrit scholar that the language of the Vedas is 'mantric' in nature, which means that the sound of the spoken word infuses the hearer with meaning and understanding, a sound which produces the desired effect as it works directly on the "substance of being." We may suggest, therefore, that the recitation of the Veda influences the soul just as a mantra is used in meditation to quiet the mind. As Le Meé says, Sanskrit recitation produces a "fine attunement."[6]

The Rig Veda, first among the Vedas, is divided into a series of six hymns. The Hymn of Man is the third and it begins with the following introduction:

Man is the Purusha
Pur-usha, the dawn in the city, he who is filled with light –

---
6 Jean Le Meé, *The Rig Veda*, Jain Publishing, 2004, p. 26.

Puru-sha, filled with wisdom and eternal happiness, citizen of Heaven
Pu-rusha, whose passions are purified.
Purusha, word so fertile in resonances, which like a musical theme developed by a skillful musician, keeps unfolding its three kaleidoscopic syllables in a never ending play, in the image of creation itself.

Such is man, that primordial and eternal principle immanent in a thousand heads, a thousand eyes, and a thousand feet, Master of immortality, Sacrificer, sacrifice and its object, origin and end of all that is – Absolute

From the point of view of analysis, this stanza is really all we need. The rest, as they say following Plato's Works, is footnotes. In the final two lines we see the core of what the principle of soul will develop through much of human history, with only a few exceptions, as we shall see. The soul is that essence of the "primordial and eternal principle" which will take many forms in myriad texts and oral traditions from native peoples to the most erudite philosophers and theologians. In addition, poets, painters, composers, dancers, indeed all the arts, will portray this essence in their own medium. The ending word, Absolute, is synonymous with God, Lord, and the One. The Absolute is *satchitananda*, where Sat is Being, Chit is consciousness and Ananda is Bliss. Our true nature then is Being Consciousness Bliss.

2. THE UPANISHADS
This formulation is also found in the Upanishads, where the word 'soul' appears overtly in the text and in the commentary, the latter

being crucial to Western understanding. We will be using for our own understanding *The Upanishads* translated from the Sanskrit by Paramananda. And for the purpose of this exploration, we focus on the Isa-Upanishad, which as Paramananda explains concerns the *"Oneness of the Soul and God, and the value of both faith and works as means of ultimate attainment are the leading themes of this Upanishad. The general teaching of the Upanishads is that works alone, even the highest, can bring only temporary happiness and must inevitably bind a man unless through them he gains knowledge of his real Self. To help him acquire this knowledge is the aim of this and all Upanishads."*[7]

The comment from Paramananda links the Upanishads to Advaita Vedanta, the early Hindu philosophy of non-duality which is based on the principle of the Oneness of the soul and God. This expression probably marks the earliest written reference to soul outside of early Egyptian hieroglyphs which reference Ka and Ba, two very different senses of the soul and the least known to later thinking. For us, the Isa-Upanishad and its links to Vedanta carry the most significant early meaning from the East to the West.

The confusion that often accompanies this text concerns the difference between the lower case self and the upper case Self. The lower case 'self' refers to the separate sense of the self, or ego consciousness. The key word here is 'separate' because it is this personal self that is not related to a larger spiritual connection to the cosmos or to Divinity. In Vedanta, on the other hand, the larger Self corresponds to the Sanskrit divinity Atman, which is also the identity of the soul within what Vedanta calls our true nature. In

---

[7] Swami Paramananda (2014-06-01). The Upanishads (p. 1). Wilder Publications, Inc.. Kindle Edition.

its simplest sense, the task of the individual is to move from the ignorance of the lower self to the knowledge of the higher, with the soul being the object of contemplation and knowledge.

In verse VIII, we have a description of the higher Self:

He (the Self) is all-encircling, resplendent, bodiless, spotless, without sinews, pure, untouched by sin, all-seeing, all-knowing, transcendent, self-existent; He has disposed all things duly for eternal years.

This description encompasses the soul as well, giving us that remnant of paradise to carry beyond the paradise of Eden into the world of pain and mortality. In another aspect, the Vedanta speaks of the notion of *tat twam asi*, or Thou Are That, meaning that we are in essence that higher Self which can be found within. Paramananda speaks in his commentary about the way in which the individual is able to gain knowledge of this Self:

In the subsequent verses Vidyâ and Avidyâ are used in something the same sense as "faith" and "works" in the Christian Bible; neither alone can lead to the ultimate goal, but when taken together they carry one to the Highest. Work done with unselfish motive purifies the mind and enables man to perceive his undying nature. From this he gains inevitably a knowledge of God, because the Soul and God are one and inseparable; and when he knows himself to be one with the Supreme and Indestructible Whole, he realizes his immortality.

Paramananda then takes us to the Katha Upanishad and has this to say in the way of an Introduction:

Pre-history, The Rig Veda and Vedanta

The Katha-Upanishad is probably the most widely known of all the Upanishads. It was early translated into Persian and through this rendering first made its way into Europe. Later Raja Ram Mohun Roy brought out an English version. It has since appeared in various languages; and English, German and French writers are all agreed in pronouncing it one of the most perfect expressions of the religion and philosophy of the Vedas. Sir Edwin Arnold popularized it by his metrical rendering under the name of "The Secret of Death," and Ralph Waldo Emerson gives its story in brief at the close of his essay on "Immortality."

The reference to Emerson here is instructive because it allows us to see how the Vedanta philosophy makes its way in the Nineteenth Century to the New England Transcendentalists. In his essay on "Immortality" Emerson found that the following text was the most effective description of the task we face in conceiving of a path to knowledge of immortality. Of all the texts and scriptures available to him, he chose this passage from the Katha. Here is Emerson leading up to the quoted passage:

A great integrity makes us immortal; an admiration, a deep love, a strong will, arms us above fear. It makes a day memorable. We say we lived years in that hour. It is strange that Jesus is esteemed by mankind the bringer of the doctrine of immortality. He is never once weak or sentimental; he is very abstemious of explanation, he never preaches the personal immortality whilst Plato and Cicero had both allowed themselves to overstep the stern limits of the spirit, and gratify the people with that picture.

The key to Emerson's language here is his use of the word 'integrity' in the first sentence. For Emerson, integrity meant unity, an integration of human and divine attributes in a coherent whole in order to acquire the knowledge needed to find the key. An individual with integrity is not separate from the whole, from the cosmos, nature, and the divine. It is also instructive that Emerson is critical of overstepping the limits of spirit to satisfy people's curiosity about immortality. He never did so, except in one instance he said, rather wryly "Immortality is there for people who are fit for it," a good advertisement for a spiritual fitness program. Emerson went on to say this about such a program:

> *Within every man's thought is a higher thought, – within the character he exhibits to-day, a higher character. The youth puts off the illusions of the child, the man puts off the ignorance and tumultuous passions of youth; proceeding thence puts off the egotism of manhood, and becomes at last a public and universal soul. He is rising to greater heights, but also rising to realities ; the outer relations and circumstances dying out, he entering deeper into God, God into him, until the last garment of egotism falls, and he is with God, – shares the will and the immensity of the First Cause.*

We will have more to say about Emerson's use of the word 'soul' in his Idealism, but for now, focused as we are on the Upanishads, we see him urging a maturity, a putting off the smaller self in favor of the greater Self. Here is the full passage that Emerson chose to end his essay on "Immortality."

Yama, the lord of Death, promised Nachiketas, the son of Gautama, to grant him three boons at his own choice. Nachiketas, knowing that his father Gautama was offended with him, said, " O Death! let Gautama be appeased in mind, and forget his anger against me : this I choose for the first boon." Yama said, "Through my favor, Gautama will remember thee with love as before." For the second boon, Nachiketas asks that the fire by which heaven is gained be made known to him; which also Yama allows, and says, "Choose the third boon, O Nachiketas!" Nachiketas said, there is this inquiry. Some say the soul exists after the death of man ; others say it does not exist. This I should like to know, instructed by thee. Such is the third of the boons. Yama said, "For this question, it was inquired of old, even by the gods ; for it is not easy to understand it. Subtle is its nature. Choose another boon, O Nachiketas! Do not compel me to this." Nachiketas said, " Even by the gods was it inquired. And as to what thou sayest, O Death, that it is not easy to understand it, there is no other speaker to be found like thee. There is no other boon like this." Yama said, "Choose sons and grandsons who may live a hundred years ; choose herds of cattle ; choose elephants and gold and horses ; choose the wide expanded earth, and live thyself as many years as thou listeth. Or, if thou knowest a boon like this, choose it, together with wealth and far-extending life. Be a king, O Nachiketas ! On the wide earth I will make thee the enjoyer of all desires. All those desires that are difficult to gain in the world of mortals, all those ask thou at thy pleasure ;- those fair nymphs of heaven with their chariots, with their musical instruments ; for the like of them are not to be gained by men. I will give them to thee, but do not ask the question of the state of the soul after death." Nachiketas said, "All those enjoyments are of yesterday.

With thee remain thy horses and elephants, with thee the dance and song.. If we should obtain wealth, we live only as long as thou pleasest. The boon which I choose I have said." Yama said, "One thing is good, another is pleasant. Blessed is he who takes the good, but he who chooses the pleasant loses the object of man. But thou, considering the objects of desire, hast abandoned them. These two, ignorance (whose object is what is pleasant) and knowledge (whose object is what is good), are known to be far asunder, and to lead to different goals. Believing this world exists, and not the other, the careless youth is subject to my sway. That knowledge for which thou hast asked is not to be obtained by argument. I know worldly happiness is transient, for that firm one is not to be obtained by what is not firm. The wise, by means of the union of the intellect with the soul, thinking him whom it is hard to behold, leaves both grief and joy. Thee, O Nachiketas! believe a house whose door is open to Brahma. Brahma the supreme, whoever knows him, obtains whatever he wishes. The soul is not born ; it does not die; it was not produced from any one. Nor was any produced from it. Unborn, eternal, it is not slain, though the body is slain; subtler than what is subtle, greater than what is great, sitting it goes far, sleeping it goes everywhere. Thinking the soul as unbodily among bodies, firm among fleeting things, the wise man casts off all grief. The soul cannot be gained by knowledge, not by understanding, not by manifold science. It can be obtained by the soul by which it is desired. It reveals its own truths."

I have quoted this portion of the Katha hymn at length in order to illustrate how determined the character of Nachiketas is not to be denied. He keeps insisting to be answered, unwavering in his quest to know the truth. Finally, Death (Yama) acquiesces and grants the request. What he reveals is centered in knowledge of the soul. We learn that the soul is the source of knowledge and to know the soul is to know the truth. As we near the end of the Katha text we have this observation: "Beyond the great Âtman is the Unmanifest; beyond the Unmanifest is the Purusha (the Cosmic Soul); beyond the Purusha there is nothing. That is the end, that is the final goal.

This rare affirmation of the presence of the Purusha, which we explored in the Rig Veda, as beyond the Unknown or Unmanifested universe completes the cosmology of the Eastern vision of the truth of reality. Although the human soul is identical to the Atman (greater Self) the Purusha or Cosmic Soul is beyond the unmanifest world. We are reminded of the opening verse in the Gospel of John: "In the beginning was the Word." In the Greek, Word is Logos, and we learn from the Pre-Socratic Heraclitus in 500 BCE that the Logos is infinite in nature and beyond understanding. Did Heraclitus, living along the coast of what is now Turkey, have access to the Upanishads? I would say yes, without doubt. Logos and Purusha are essentially the same.

Further, in verse XIII, we learn more about the Cosmic Soul, the Purusha:

That Purusha, of the size of a thumb, is like a light without smoke, lord of the past and the future. He is the same today and tomorrow. This verily is That.

Commentary:
In this verse the teacher defines the effulgent nature of the Soul, whose light is pure like a flame without smoke. He also answers

the question put by Nachiketas as to what happens after death, by declaring that no real change takes place, because the Soul is ever the same.

The Katha teaches the means of immortality as no other cultural text manages. The key lies in the Purusha. The teaching begins with verse XV

When all the ties of the heart are cut asunder here, then the mortal becomes immortal. Such is the teaching. There are a hundred and one nerves of the heart. One of them penetrates the centre of the head. Going upward through it, one attains immortality. The other (hundred nerve-courses) lead, in departing, to different worlds.

Commentary:
The nervous system of the body provides the channels through which the mind travels; the direction in which it moves is determined by its desires and tendencies. When the mind becomes pure and desireless, it takes the upward course and at the time of departing passes out through the imperceptible opening at the crown of the head; but as long as it remains full of desires, its course is downward towards the realms where those desires can be satisfied.

XVII
The Purusha, the inner Self, of the size of a thumb, is ever seated in the heart of all living beings. With perseverance man should draw Him out from his body as one draws the inner stalk from a blade of grass. One should know Him as pure and deathless, as pure and deathless.

Commentary:
As has been explained in Part Four, verse XII, the inner Self, although unlimited, is described as "the size of a thumb" because of its abiding-place in the heart, often likened to a lotus-bud which is similar to a thumb in size and shape. Through the process of steadfast discrimination, one should learn to differentiate the Soul from the body, just as one separates the pith from a reed.

3. The soul's five sheaths in Vedanta

Tradition in Vedanta holds that the soul, which is also the larger Self or Atman, possesses five coverings or sheaths which must be released before the Self is liberated from earthly existence. To simplify the complexity of the sheaths or Koshas as they are called, they may be described from the outer to the inner sheaths as follows: the anamaya or physical, the pranamaya or energy, the manamaya or mental, the vijnanamaya or wisdom, and the anandamaya or bliss. One by one these sheaths are stripped away until the Atman, or immortal soul, is free to continue its journey. What that journey will entail is a function of the nature of the soul as determined from its lifetime in its last embodiment.

4. Buddhism: What fits the case?

This dialogue between the Buddha and Vaccha continues the subject of the soul and its purported rebirth:

> Vaccha asks, "But Reverend Gautama, where is the person... reborn?"
> "To say that he is reborn, Vaccha, does not fit the case," replied the Buddha.
> "Then he is not reborn?"

"To say that he is not reborn does not fit the case."
"Then he is neither reborn or not reborn?"
"To say that, Vacchagotta, does not fit the case."

On the existence of the soul, Buddhism offers a special case. Essentially, Buddhism does not recognize the concept of an immortal soul connected to the person. Tradition speaks of an illusory soul. This interpretation of Buddhist writings, however, has little effect on the tradition in Buddhism of rebirth. It is just that the tradition does not speak of an individualized soul within to a person being reincarnated in another embodiment over many lifetimes. Rather, the Buddha prefers the word 'rebirth' instead, a subtle distinction but important in that since life itself as we know it is an illusion or *maya*, there cannot be a substantial soul that reincarnates.

On the subject of rebirth in Buddhism, at least in the Pali Canon of the Buddha's authentic teachings, the matter is important because the tradition says that in becoming the Buddha, Siddhartha was released from the cycle of rebirth and his consciousness would no longer exist in the cosmos. This release from rebirth signified the release from the suffering we all experience in a lifetime. And since Buddhism regards the soul as part of the human being's earthly existence, it does not survive the death of that existence.

We can understand, then, the frustrating dialogue between the Buddha and Vaccha who was unable to ask the question in the right way, using the right words. In saying, "it does not fit the case," the Buddha uses the correct philosophic phrase. "What fits the case" means what is a true or accurate statement. It is extremely difficult for a student or unenlightened person to ask the

Buddha about rebirth in such a way that the reply would be "That fits the case."

Brahman, then, the highest, deepest, final, transcendental power inhabiting the visible, tangible levels of our nature, transcends both the so-called "gross body" and the inner world of forms and experiences—the notions, ideas, thoughts, emotions, visions, fantasies, etc.—of the "subtle body". As the power that turns into and animates everything in the microcosm as well as in the outer world, it is the divine inmate of the mortal coil and is identical with the Self (Atman)—the higher aspect of that which we in the West style (indiscriminately) the "soul."

In similar fashion, mention must be made of the most ancient Chinese texts, especially the *I Ching, The Book of Changes*, which according to most sources dates from 1600 BCE or earlier and has gone through many incarnations. This ancient book of wisdom does not, on its surface, deal with human destiny in the afterlife, but mostly with earthly matters, but in 1924 a German translation by Richard Wilhelm began a re-evaluation of the *I Ching*, resulting in more universal interpretations. In fact, Wilhelm made the following evaluation of the text after working on his translation: "The relentless mechanization and rationalization of life in the West needs the Eastern adhesion to a natural profundity of soul."[8]

---

8 Eliot Weinberger, NY Review of Books, Feb. 26, 2016.

CHAPTER 3

Egypt and Reincarnation

THE TITLE OF this chapter, to be devoted to the presence of soul in early Egyptian belief and practice, is so named from the section in the book *The Shape of Ancient Thought* by Thomas McEvilley, whose task in life was to convince the academic establishment that the infusion of tradition, insight and knowledge in early history traveled extensively from East to West and back again with the result that what we traditionally think of as distinct and separate traditions were nothing of the kind. And this exploration of the soul will accept his insights because they are both sound and logical.

In the case of Egypt, also a part of this infusion of influence, what we had available to us in writing of its early history, was the work of a Greek, Herodotus, who lived during the fifth century, BCE (c. 484–425 BC) and was a contemporary of Pericles. During his lifetime, he traveled to Egypt and according to his testimony studied with the temple priests.

What is important to remember is that the time of his travels in Egypt was during what we call the Late Period of Egyptian history, and it was a time of significant decline and conflict. In fact, this period was during the so-called twenty-seventh dynasty when Egypt was part of the Persian Empire. As a result, we cannot be certain about the testimony of the priests during the visits of Herodotus. Nonetheless, here is what he wrote on the matter of the soul in Egyptian religion:

> *Such as think the tales told by the Egyptians credible are free to accept them for history. For my own part, I propose to myself throughout my whole work faithfully to record the traditions of the several nations. The Egyptians maintain that Ceres and Bacchus preside in the realms below. They were also the first to broach the opinion that the soul of man is immortal and that, when the body dies, it enters into the form of an animal which is born at the moment, thence passing on from one animal into another, until it has circled through the forms of all the creatures which tenant the earth, the water, and the air, after which it enters again into a human frame, and is born anew. The whole period of the transmigration is (they say) three thousand years. There are Greek writers, some of an earlier, some of a later date, who have borrowed this doctrine from the Egyptians, and put it forward as their own. I could mention their names, but I abstain from doing so.*[9]

The testimony is clear enough in asserting the presence of an immortal soul as part of human nature. As we will learn later, this testimony takes on greater credibility and clarity in the Hermetic tradition, which was formulated from Egyptian, Greek and Early Christian scholars in the Second and Third Centuries CE., but well before the discovery of the Rosetta Stone in 1799 and its translation by Jean-Fransois Champollion in 1822. After that date, when Egyptologists had had a chance to study the hieroglyphics on temple walls, obelisks and tombs, the testimony of

---
9 *Herodotus, History, Book 1*

Herodotus was thoroughly dismissed. No, the scholars insisted, the Egyptians did not subscribe to reincarnation, although they did have a complex understanding of the soul.

As we shall see in the next chapter on the Greeks, the Indic tradition of reincarnation had influence in the Greek mysteries, and at least some of that tradition came as well from the Egyptians. Here is McEvilley on the Egyptians: "...they had a number of traits in their religious lore that should be called reincarnationistic and some of them seem to have entered the Greek milieu. As Jane Ellen Harrison said: 'The Greeks need not have borrowed it from Egypt, and yet it is probable that the influence of Egypt… helped out the doctrine.'"[10]

The reason that the issue of reincarnation of the soul is relevant to the overall discussion of its nature and destiny is that when we get to the Christian orthodoxy on the soul, where reincarnation is dismissed as false, the overall acceptance of it as part of the soul's nature will be present for our consideration.

To explore the argument further, here is a passage from McEvilley on the subject of reincarnation and transformation from the Pyramid texts in the Egyptian Books of the Dead:

The Egyptian Pyramid Texts and Books of the Dead contain numerous elements which may have formed part of the background for the development of the doctrine of reincarnation. One of these is the shape-changing which the deceased goes through in the afterlife. In this process there is a reincarnating entity (an entity that changes from one body to another, which can be called the "soul" in a looser, pre-Platonic sense), and in its afterlife

---

10 McEvilley, Thomas (2012-02-07). The Shape of Ancient Thought (p. 129). Skyhorse Publishing. Kindle Edition.

adventures, this entity has the power to go through many transformations, passing into human and animal and other forms. Chapter titles in the Papyrus of Ani include "The Chapter of Changing into a Golden Hawk," "The Chapter of Changing into a Lotus," "The Chapter of Changing into a Crocodile," "The Chapter of Changing into a Heron," and others of the same type. In his more recent, but less complete, translation (which is provided here in endnotes) Faulkner renders the verb in these titles "Being Transformed Into." The view that these "changing" or "transforming" activities might be considered rebirths that occur in the afterlife was held early in the century by Schayer, who argued that the Egyptian verb in question has an ordinary meaning of "be born." "The spells of the Book of the Dead were supposed to make it possible for the dead to be reborn in any form he desired in the hereafter." When the reincarnating entity changes its form or species, in other words, the event could be described as a redeath-and-rebirth-in-the-afterlife. In India the doctrine of reincarnation, in an early stage of its development, posited rebirths and redeaths in the afterlife, emphasizing a desire to avoid the redeaths. Similarly in the Book of the Dead, Papyrus of Ani, one chapter is entitled "The Chapter of Not Dying a Second Time."

Reincarnation aside, our traditional knowledge of Egyptian spiritual life and practice centers on mummification and the afterlife. Ever since Howard Carter's discovery of King Tut's tomb in 1923, interest in the afterlife among the ancient Egyptians has been great. In the common awareness of most people, the issue of the afterlife seemed to focus on the Pharaohs and perhaps the others among Egypt's elite.

The Soul's Journey

However, the more esoteric traditions offer a broader and more vital history. As I was researching this material, I pulled from my shelf a copy of John Anthony West's *Travelers Key to Ancient Egypt*, and on the flyleaf was the following inscription: "For Richard and Astrid, inscribed in the King's Chamber of the Great Pyramid, at 12:30 PM, 11/17/03, John Anthony West."

My wife and I were coming to the end of a three week trip to Egypt with John Anthony, and on the next-to-last day, before flying out of Cairo, we were given the privilege of spending two hours in the King's Chamber by ourselves. The lights and the loud ventilation fans were turned off, and we were left to sit quietly and feel the presence of five thousand years of human existence in that space. The mystery of the space was evident, and we were strongly moved by knowing that here had been people like Plato and Napoleon and how many other seekers after spiritual knowledge. In that space, John spoke about the concept of the Egyptian soul.

Taken from the Travelers Key here is some of what he said:

> *Egyptian religion as the science of spiritual transformation described the development and interaction of more than half a dozen different spiritual elements and bodies, the components of the inner man. To the Egyptians these elements were as distinct as hydrogen, carbon, and oxygen are to modern material science.*

Ba is usually translated as "soul" which unfortunately means something different to everybody. Ba is the animating principle, the vital or divine spark that vivifies all sentient creatures. When the Ba departs, the body dies. The *Ba* is immortal and individual only in the sense that it animates this or that particular body over the course of its existence. The *Ba* is depicted as a human-headed bird, an interesting reversal of the usual practice in which certain of the *neterw* are drawn with human bodies and animal heads. The glyph for the word *Ba* is a heron or stork. Sometimes the *Ba* is shown as a stork, sometimes as a falcon. Since the stork's most salient characteristic is its migrating and homing instinct, its choice to represent the *Ba* strongly suggests the notion of reincarnation, though academic Egyptologists do not customarily put this interpretation upon it.

Ka, the other term for soul, is usually rendered as the "double," which means nothing to anybody, but no other single word captures this complex conception either. *Ka* is the power that fixes and makes individual the animating spirit that is *Ba*. *Ka* is the complex of attractive or magnetic powers whose result is what today we would call personality: the pervading sense of "I" that inhabits the body but that is not the body. (the "I" may be present even when the sense of body is lost entirely as in total paralysis or certain kinds of anesthesia.) The *Ka* is complex. There is the animal *Ka* concerned with the desires of the body; the divine *Ka* that heeds the call of the spirit; and the intermediate *Ka*, which provides the impetus to those on the path for gradually gaining control of the animal *Ka* and placing it in the service of the divine *Ka*. The *Ka* does not die with the mortal body, though it may break into its many constituent aspects. If the symbolist view of reincarnation is correct, then it is the *Ka* that reincarnates, a magnetic center or locus of qualities that survives physical death and that requires another physical vehicle in order to continue the work of self-perfection.

If during life on earth, the *Ka* has degenerated to the point where it has been divested of all virtue, of everything truly human,

The Soul's Journey

then it does not reincarnate, and the *Ka* disperses into the various lower animal and vegetable realms. This is the second death the Egyptian texts speak of with such fear and horror. It may be this understanding that lies behind the curious doctrine of metempsychosis in which the deceased may be reborn as an animal or even a bush or tree.

The statues of the deceased placed in the tomb and the long funerary texts and the walls filled with carved reliefs or paintings are all devices designed to focus the *Ka* of the deceased on the task of further spiritual development.

The glyph for the *Ka* is a pair of arms outstretched towards heaven, emphasizing its function as attractive or magnetic power. Sometimes the *Ka* of the king is shown as a statue or drawing of the king with the sign of the *Ka* on top of his head. In other instances, the ram-headed potter, Khnum, is depicted fashioning the body of the king and an identical figure, his *Ka*, on the potter's wheel, which is no doubt what has prompted the *Ka* to be translated as the "double."

The perfected man, to achieve immortality, united his *Ka* to his *Ba*: his individual essence to the divine spark within. Apart from the frequently depicted *Ba* and *Ka*, the human being included a number of other entities or powers. The body was *khat*, a word meaning 'the corruptible' and the *khu*, which was a luminous body associated with the gods but also appearing within the elevated human being.

The *akh*, another spiritual entity which "was the transfigured spirit that survived death and mingled with the gods."[18] One source explained that the akh was only allowed to individuals whose souls were worthy because they were good people in their past lives. Condemned criminals did not have proper burials and their real names were buried with them. So it was believed criminals could not survive in the afterlife and the criminal could not become or have an *akh*. "An *akh* is the blessed or 'transfigured' soul of a person who died and whose soul had been judged by Osiris and found justified. An *akh* was an effective spirit, one could still influence events in this world." The *akh* and *Ka* were believed to need a preserved body and tomb in order to exist.

What emerges from the complexity of the Egyptian conceptions of soul is the priestly time and effort given to matters of the afterlife, including of course mummification. The complexity also reflected the interest in cosmology and the human connection to the universe. The Egyptians were world-class astronomers and educated the rest of the Mediterranean world with the mysteries of stars and planets and mathematical investigations of the Earth and its movements.

It is in this sense that the *History* of Herodotus is important as an early guide to the influences of Egyptian culture on the cultures of Greece, Persia. and Rome. We also find several passages in the *Book of the Dead* dwelling on the soul's eternal nature in ways that seem to suggest the idea reported by Herodotus that the soul is infused through all of nature. The deceased being asks: "How long ... have I to live?" One answer was "It is decreed that you shall live for millions of millions of years." The continuation of the passage foreshadows the Orphic myth of the soul's return, after expiating its crimes, to the company of the gods. The deceased being asks: "May it be granted to me that I pass on to the holy princes, for indeed I am doing away with all the wrong which I did, from the time when this earth came into being."

The Soul's Journey

In this passage it may seem that the millions of millions of years refer to the afterlife in eternity attained after "doing away with all the wrong which I did." This clearly is the meaning when it is said of Osiris Ani in the Papyrus of Ani, "he shall do whatsover pleaseth him, as [do] the gods who are in the underworld, for everlasting millions of ages, world without end." But other passages place the millions of millions of years in the soul's past rather than its future. Typically the soul, its memory expanded somehow, realizes that it has lived for countless ages rather than for a single, finite lifetime.

In a side note, we who live a time-centered lifetime worry about existing in eternity, wondering what there will be to do with all that "time." But since eternity has no time, there will be no question either about "doing something." As Woody Allen once remarked: "I don't worry about heaven at all, except I do wonder if they'll be able to break a twenty." Such is the nature of our sense of imaginative dislocation that we can't fathom eternal life.

The soul's recognition of its own primeval nature, its recollection that it has lived since before time and will live endless ages more, seems a part of the "glorification" in form that indicates Ani is ready to "get thee to the heights of heaven" and "pass on to the holy princes." The idea is substantially the same as Plato's belief that the soul, in the afterlife, recalls its true nature as eternal and universal, and is also substantially the same as the Hindu idea that the soul can recognize its own identity with the Universal Self and by this recognition pass into the Self forever.

But what was the soul doing for these millions of millions of years before it was ready to return to heaven? Although there is no overt mention of reincarnation, it seems that the soul has been purified somehow through living for millions of years; whether it is automatically purified by time or purifies itself by special efforts is not made clear. It is also unclear whether the soul (like the fravashi in Mazdaism) has waited in heaven for those millions of years before its descent upon earth, or whether the descent itself took place millions of years ago. In an especially suggestive passage, Osiris says: ... my soul is eternity. I am the creator of darkness, and I appoint unto it a resting place in the uttermost parts of heaven. I am the prince of eternity, I am the exalted one [in] Nebu. I grow young in [my] city, I grow young in my homestead. My name is "Never failing." My name is "Soul, Creator of Nu, who maketh his abode in the underworld." My nest is not seen, and I have not broken my egg. I am lord of millions of years. I have made my nest in the uttermost parts of heaven. I have come down unto the earth of Seb. I have done away with my faults." The soul has lived forever, according to this passage since even before the primeval ocean, and its descent upon the earth was in order to "do away with its faults."

As in both Orphic and Upanisadic contexts, the descent to earth (i.e., into a mortal body) is seen as a punishment or purificatory austerity after which the soul may reclaim its place in heaven. Its possession of the kingship seems a sign of this readiness. Empedocles' doctrine that those in their final incarnations are princes and other mighty figures in the community may derive from this pharaonic tradition: To be reborn at last as pharaoh is to be at the end of the cycle, to have access to the Osiris principle again.

That the Egyptian religious experience included reincarnation seems evident from the references in the Book of the Dead and in the overall infusion of such themes streaming into the

The Soul's Journey

Mediterranean basin from the East. McEvilley summarizes the principle in the following outline of the principle:

As the Bronze Age turned into the Iron Age, many common assumptions about life were revised—among them, views of the afterlife. In the Early Iron Age, by about the seventh or the sixth century B.C., a kind of soup of afterlife beliefs—including rebirth in the afterlife, transcendent rebirth, redeath in the afterlife, rebirth in this life, redeath in this life, permanent heavens and hells, temporary heavens and hells, and various combinations of these elements—swirled around Egypt, Mesopotamia, Persia, Greece, India, and elsewhere. Out of this soup the Tripartite Doctrine of Reincarnation emerged as one more or less permanent solution, the Zoroastrian belief in permanent heavens and hells as another. The evidence suggests that the tripartite doctrine developed in India and diffused thence to Greece. It also points to the Egyptian Osiris cult as an influence at some fairly early stage. One early type of reincarnation doctrine—perhaps connected with a myth of cyclical time—that seems to have been known in India, in Egypt, and perhaps in Greece (to Herodotus, at least), involved the necessary reembodiment of the soul in every available life-form before it is reborn as a human and returns to the company of the gods. Reincarnation as a process of being reborn throughout all of nature may be an earlier form—perhaps a Bronze Age form—that was displaced in the Early Iron Age by different cultic versions of the new idea of early escape. This development would be part of a general trend in which Bronze Age communalism was replaced by Iron Age individualism. In the version in which the reincarnating entity is processed through all of nature, its purification consists in a relentless one-step-at-a-time universalization which gradually wears away all particular points of view. In the later doctrine featuring the goal of early release, an additional type of purification is required that consists in individual ascetic and moral exertions taken on in addition to the step-by-step universalization and having the ability to speed it up and finish ahead of schedule.

In sum, following the analysis in McEvilley's text, we can say that the general belief through centuries of Egyptian culture offers a philosophy of reincarnation which posits an evolution of existences in which a soul undergoes a process of recovery from a life of waste and ignorance to a life of knowledge and growth in relation to higher principles until it is released from incarnations and merges into a unity with the gods or higher beings.

Given this summary, we move now to explore the Greek vision of the soul to see what influence the Egyptian beliefs had on the Greek soul or psyche.

CHAPTER 4

Greece and the Psyche

THE PHILOSOPHER KARL Jaspers termed the years from 800 BCE to 200 BCE The Axial Age throughout the known world for its dramatic birth of great teachings which transformed the way human beings understood themselves. The Greeks in particular moved dramatically from the Archaic to the Classical to the Hellenic periods in their own culture, stimulated first by Homer's epics and by Hesiod's cosmology, then by the Pre-Socratic genius of Pythagoras, Heraclitus, Parmenides and Anaxagoras and finally by the philosophies of Plato and Aristotle.

In this brief 600-year revolution of thought and knowledge, ideas about the psyche or soul evolved and were continuously transformed by the influences not only of philosophy but by the brilliance of Greek tragedy, the construction of inspiring temples, the myths of the Olympian gods, the dramatic experiment with democracy, and the power of the ancient mysteries of Delphi and Eleusis.

The idea of the soul in the Archaic Period, through the works of Homer and Hesiod, centered on the idea of the life force. The psyche meant life itself. When the body died, the psyche became a shade or shadow in the Underworld, where Hades dwelled with his bride Persephone. The myth of Orpheus and Eurydice was a powerful affirmation of the nature of human existence in its relationship to life and death. Its tale of lost love and the rule of life and death defined the psyche in human nature.

However, for the ordinary person, this fate was fraught with sadness and anxiety, and past of the culture in ancient times was the presence of several famous Oracles of the Dead, one of which is located in Cumae, Italy, where visitors today can go to see how the living could commune with their loved ones in the underworld. These places were perhaps more commonly visited in much the same way as we visit cemeteries with flowers on Memorial Day. However, the ceremonies attended in the Oracles of the Dead were extensive, long lasting and arduous. At the same time there grew up a more elevated spiritual participation known as Orphism.

The following is a useful description by Will Durant of the essentials of Orphism and its relevance to the evolution of the soul:

Between 700 and 600 BC there came into Hellas, from Egypt, Thrace, and Thessaly, another mystic cult. Orphicism was derived from the story of Orpheus, a Thracian who surpassed all men in music and culture. He often is referred to as a musician, sometimes as a priest of Dionysus. He played the lyre so well, and sang to it so melodiously, that those who heard him almost began to worship him as a god; wild animals became tame at his voice, and trees and rocks left their places to follow the sound of his harp. He married the fair Eurydice, and almost went mad when death took her. He plunged into Hades, charmed Persephone with his lyre, and was allowed to lead Eurydice up to life again on the condition that he would not look back upon her until the surface of the earth was reached. At the last barrier anxiety overcame himself she should no longer be following; he looked back, only to see her snatched down once more into the nether world. Thracian women, resenting his unwillingness to console himself with them, tore him to pieces in one of their Dionysian revels. He left behind many sacred songs; by 520 BC these hymns had acquired a sacred character as divinely inspired, and formed the basis of a mystical cult related to that of Dionysus but far superior to it in doctrine, ritual, and moral influence.

The creed was essentially the affirmation of the passion (suffering), death, and resurrection of the divine son of Dionysus, and resurrection of all men into a future of reward and punishment. Since the Titans, who had slain Dionysus, were believed to have been the ancestors of man, a taint of original sin rested upon all humanity; and in punishment for this the soul was inclosed in the body as in a prison or a tomb. But man might be consoled by knowing that the Titans had eaten Dionysus, and that therefore every man harbored, in his soul, a particle of indestructible divinity In a mystic sacrament of communion the ORPHIC worshipers ate the raw flesh of a bull as a symbol of Dionysus to commemorate the slaying and eating of the god, and to absorb the divine essence anew. After death, according to Orphic theology, the soul goes down to Hades, and must face judgment by the gods of the underworld; the Orphic hymns and ritual instructed the faithful in the act of preparing for this comprehensive and final examination. If the verdict was guilty, there would be severe punishment. One form of the doctrine conceived this punishment as eternal, and transmitted to later theology the notion of hell. Another form adopted the idea of transmigration: the soul was reborn again and again into lives happier or bitterer than before according to the purity or impurity of its former existence; and this wheel of rebirth would turn until complete purity was achieved, and the soul was admitted to the Islands of the Blest. Another variant offered hope that the punishment in Hades might be ended through penances performed in advance by the individual, or, after his death, by his friends. In the way a doctrine of purgatory and indulgences arose. And thus there were in Orphism trends that culminated in the morals and monasticism of Christianity. The reckless looseness of the Olympians was replaced by a strict code of conduct; a conception of sin and conscience, a dualistic view of the body as evil and of the soul as divine, entered into Greek thought; subjugation of the flesh became a main purpose of religion, as a condition of release for the soul.

The influence of the sect was extensive and enduring. Perhaps it was here that Pythagoreans took their diet, their dress, and their theory of transmigration; Plato, though he rejected much of Orphism, accepted its opposition of body and soul, its puritan tendency, its hope of immortality. Part of the pantheism and asceticism of Stoicism may be traced to an Orphic origin. The Neo-Platonists of Alexandria possessed a large collection of Orphic writings, and based upon them much of their theology and their mysticism. The doctrines of hell, purgatory, and heaven, of the body versus the soul, of the divine son slain and reborn, as well as the sacramental eating of the body and the blood and divinity of the god, directly or deviously influenced Christianity, which was itself a mystery religion of atonement and hope, of mystic union and release. The basic ideas and ritual of the Orphic cult are alive and flourishing amongst us today.[11]

---

11 Will Durant, *The Life of Greece*, vol. 2 of The Story of Civilization, Simon and Schuster, 1966, 188-92.

The importance of the Orphic tradition is its potential as a theology, that is, the study of divine things, a spiritual cosmology. Although the figure of Orpheus is bound up with the Olympian gods, his spiritual influence and nature drew him close to the people, particularly in the account of his loss of the love of his life. Whereas the Olympians took their many sexual exploits in stride and moved on, Orpheus suffered from the loss and his guilt for not being obedient and for glancing back at Eurydice, who was drawn back forever in the underworld.

In addition to the Greek source and character of the sect, scholars have found connections to Vedanta and Egypt as well, conferring a more universal significance to Orphism.

However, at the same time that sects like Orphism were spreading through the Greek world, the natural philosophers were attempting to explain the natural world. Pythagoras made great strides in mathematics and the principles behind musical harmony. He included in his teaching the Eastern traditions of reincarnation, taught his students a new sense of the psyche as an immortal element existing within human nature. It was more than the life force; it possessed a connection to the divine, to Being itself.

Following that impulse, Heraclitus of Ephesus in Ionia on the coast of what is now Turkey, developed the principle of the Logos, the law ordering the cosmos. He said, "Listening not to me but to the Logos, it is wise to believe that all things are One. His sense of the Logos would be felt 600 years later when Saint John would say, "In the beginning was the Logos," or Word or power of creation itself in the person of the risen Christ.

The Logos for Heraclitus was a universal force and presence. It had spiritual essence. As such it also was present within the human being. When he said "Listen not to me but to the Logos..." he meant that the Logos lived within each person and could be heard if the individual was awake. Fragments number one and nine make the case:

1. *The Logos, which is as I describe, proves incomprehensible, both before it is heard and even after it is heard. For although all things happen according to the Logos, many act as if they have no experience of it, even when they do experience such words and action as I explain, as when I separate out each thing according to its nature and state how it is; but as to the rest, they fail to notice what they do after they wake up, just as they forget what they do when they sleep.*
9. *We have as One in us that which is living and dead, waking and sleeping, young and old: because these having transformed are those, and those having transformed are these.*

Through statements like these Heraclitus opened the door to a connection between the material and divine worlds in his teaching. This connection existed in the Orphic mysteries as well, but Heraclitus made the connection more philosophical than allegorical.

On the western frontier of Greek influence Parmenides of Elea on the Italian boot, would give the Greeks a sense of Being and relate the psyche to that eternal presence. Parmenides may have been the most insightful and spiritual of the Pre-Socratics. He was so revered by the people of Elea that history records the epithet "a Parmenidean life" in his honor. His famous poem describing Being and its essence has the following teaching describing in allegorical language the intuitive insight into the meaning of Being as manifested in his soul:

> *The goddess receives me with kind words;*
> *Taking my right hand in hers, she addresses me:*
> *"Youth, attended as you are by immortal ones,*
> *Brought here by the mares to my dwelling place,*
> *Welcome! No evil destiny has drawn you here,*
> *So very far from human habitation.*
>
> *It is by divine command and right that you have come.*
> *You shall inquire into everything, into the vast unmoving*
> *Heart of well-rounded Truth, and also into the opinions*
> *Of mortals, where Truth cannot reside. Even so,*
> *You will learn opinion as well, to move through*
> *Those things that merely seem, to learn to test them.*

What could be a clearer metaphor of the soul's gift of insight. The image resembles what we shall find in the hermetic materials nearly a thousand years later. Plato was sufficiently moved by this poem that he devoted an entire dialogue entitled "The Parmenides" in honor of Parmenides in order to emphasize the idea of the dialectic as crucial to progress in the acquisition of wisdom. Here the older and wiser Parmenides addresses the young Socrates:

> *Socrates, [you are] attempting to define the beautiful, the just, the good, and the ideas generally, without sufficient previous training. I noticed your deficiency, when I heard you talking here with your friend Aristoteles, the day before yesterday. The*

impulse that carries you towards philosophy is assuredly noble and divine; but there is an art which is called by the vulgar idle talking, and which is often imagined to be useless; in that you must train and exercise yourself, now that you are young, or truth will elude your grasp.

The art of which Parmenides speaks is the science Plato uses to penetrate ignorance; it is accompanied by the art of looking within after calming the mind from its constant tendency to wander and opinionate. That art rests in the soul, there to be found in quiet moments, alone. As Emerson expressed it, "When the act of reflection takes place in the mind, and we look at ourselves in the light of thought, we discover that our life is embosomed in beauty."

The act of reflection after the discipline of the dialectic takes place in the mind, and it was the powerful concept of the greater Mind brought to Athens in the fifth century BCE by Anaxagoras, who was, surprisingly, the first philosopher to teach in Athens. Prior to his arrival to tutor the young Pericles, the work of the natural philosophers would not have been tolerated by the entrenched hierarchy of priest and officials of the Olympian order. The fact that Anaxagoras survived as long as he did was a testimony to the power of Pericles when he became the head of state.

Anaxagoras proclaimed the existence of Nous, or Mind, as a universal source and divine connection to human life and the psyche. His concept of Mind joined the Logos of Heraclitus and the Being of Parmenides in a trinity of divine order, which when it was understood and merged with knowledge of the new human order gave credence to a deeper theological and psychological awareness of human potential and reality. This knowledge would find its champion in a mature Socrates and then transferred to Plato.

These three principles – Logos, Being and Mind – gave to the soul a new identity within the human instrument. As a result, the ancient mysteries of the Delphic oracle and the annual celebration of the Eleusinean Mysteries lent a new and fresh meaning to the psyche. The famous saying Know Thyself inscribed in the temple of Apollo at Delphi, inspired a new sense of self-knowledge and self-awareness, which was reflected in the famous Allegory of the Cave in Plato's "Republic." And the mysteries at Eleusis celebrating the rebirth of Dionysus, replicating the similar account of Osiris in Egypt, gave the psyche an immortal nature of greater emphasis then the Archaic shadow existence in Hades.

But it is mostly in the Hellenic Period, with the founding of Plato's Academy and then Aristotle's Lyceum that we find a greater sophistication in the nature of the soul, an understanding that when Paul came to preach the "Good News" of the Christian message to the Greeks, they and then the Romans following suit came to accept the Christian message.

This brief survey of the rapid evolution of the soul among the elite Greeks needs amplification before we can grasp the full sense of the psyche as it found itself in Christian hands. When Socrates was wandering in the marketplace, or Agora) in Athens, questioning anyone who would speak with him about the nature of reality and truth, he would explore the moral and ethical principles of human life, not as they appeared in law or tradition, but as they appeared in daily life. He reported that whenever he had to act or make an important decision, an inner voice, a moral center within would speak to him, but the only thing it ever said was "No." This sense of what we think of as conscience, was part of the psyche. It was a feeling that arose when he was on the verge of doing wrong, suggesting that as human beings we have an innate sense of right and wrong as part of our nature. Many contemporary writers and thinkers equate the soul with the conscience.

This inner tuning of our moral nature was an added quality of psychic identity and became tied to the afterlife and to Plato's description of the soul's journey after death. As an example of that journey, here is part of the description of that journey in the final section of the "Republic." The story involves the account from Homer of the warrior Er, who was slain in battle, placed on the funereal pyre only to come alive and report the journey of his soul, as follows:

> *He said that when his soul left the body he went on a journey with a great company, and that they came to a mysterious place at which there were two openings in the earth; they were near together, and over against them were two other openings in the heaven above. In the intermediate space there were judges seated, who commanded the just, after they had given judgment on them and had bound their sentences in front of them, to ascend by the heavenly way on the right hand; and in like manner the unjust were bidden by them to descend by the lower way on the left hand; these also bore the symbols of their deeds, but fastened on their backs. He drew near, and they told him that he was to be the messenger who would carry the report of the other world to men, and they bade him hear and see all that was to be heard and seen in that place. Then he beheld and saw on one side the souls departing at either opening of heaven and earth when sentence had been given on them; and at the two other openings other souls, some ascending out of the earth dusty and worn with travel, some descending out of heaven clean and bright. And arriving ever and*

The Soul's Journey

anon they seemed to have come from a long journey, and they went forth with gladness into the meadow, where they encamped as at a festival; and those who knew one another embraced and conversed, the souls which came from earth curiously enquiring about the things above, and the souls which came from heaven about the things beneath. And they told one another of what had happened by the way, those from below weeping and sorrowing at the remembrance of the things which they had endured and seen in their journey beneath the earth (now the journey lasted a thousand years), while those from above were describing heavenly delights and visions of inconceivable beauty. The story, Glaucon, would take too long to tell; but the sum was this:--He said that for every wrong which they had done to any one they suffered tenfold; or once in a hundred years--such being reckoned to be the length of man's life, and the penalty being thus paid ten times in a thousand years. If, for example, there were any who had been the cause of many deaths, or had betrayed or enslaved cities or armies, or been guilty of any other evil behaviour, for each and all of their offences they received punishment ten times over, and the rewards of beneficence and justice and holiness were in the same proportion.

Plato's use of allegory and myth in his otherwise rational texts serves as a valuable connection between the Homeric world of the Archaic and the more inner-directed rational world of the Hellenic, and is also an indication of how and why the Greek peoples strongly embraced the Christian message when it finally arrived over 400 years later. The power of myth still influences religious belief in most cultures, and stories about the journey of the soul are many and, for the most part, appealing.

It is in fact rare, but not totaling absent, that rational approaches to the nature of soul are without mythological coloring. Indeed how can we talk about soul without animating its nature and presence with metaphor? Therefore, it is not surprising that Plato offers allegory in some places to illustrate a principle.

The truth is, however, that when we want to learn about the nature of the soul, Plato and Aristotle are not our most valuable resources. Plato wants to save Athens, to establish an ideal state after a disastrous war with Sparta, a war where values and human life shattered the dream of a city-state where justice and the Good could rule. He was less interested in an afterlife of glory or punishment except as it might help to maintain a just society.

That said, Plato was also the student of Socrates, who was more the guru than his student Plato. Socrates was most certainly influenced by Eastern thought and was given to meditation and listening to his soul. The Allegory of the Cave is pure Socrates, an exercise in soul waking and enlightenment. The prisoner who is released from bondage in the shadow world of illusion, struggles up and out of the cave into the light, there to see reality and then with that realization to lead a self-aware life listening to his inner voice.

The death of his teacher Socrates when Plato was just a young man was a profound blow and drove him out of Athens to go we know not where, and when he returned, he set up his Academy a mile away from the scene of the Agora where Socrates drank the hemlock. The Academy was devoted to the Pythagorean principles of geometry and self-study. The nature of the soul was of course relevant to that pursuit and in dialogues like the "Phaedo" and "Timaeus" is treated but not as directly or in as great depth as we would find centuries later in Plotinus.

The Soul's Journey

In the famous Seventh Letter, generally agreed to be genuine, Plato said that nothing that he wrote and published had any resemblance to the actual teaching in the Academy, to the work on the self that occurred there in the Pythagorean-like secrecy of its daily work. The speculation is that it was the teaching of Socrates that occupied the Academy and kept the critics away from the door, leaving those who entered the sanctuary free from heresy and politics.

The traditional view of Plato's work and overall purpose centers on the *polis*, or ideal state. In that state the ideals of the soul were the same as the structure of the *polis*. For Plato the soul had a tripartite structure, the elements of which he named as the spiritual, the rational, and the appetitive. The traditional interpretation of this structure is usually defined as follows:

> *The spirited soul (will or volition) is the active portion; its function is to carry out the dictates of reason in practical life, courageously doing whatever the intellect has determined to be best.*
>
> *The rational soul (mind or intellect) is the thinking portion within each of us, which discerns what is real and not merely apparent, judges what is true and what is false, and wisely makes the rational decisions in accordance with which human life is most properly lived. Finally, the appetitive soul (emotion or desire) is the portion of each of us that wants and feels many things, most of which must be deferred in the face of rational pursuits if we are to achieve a salutary degree of self-control.*[12]

The goals of the state, with its philosopher king, its warrior class and its ordinary citizens, had to possess the qualities of the

---

12   http://www.philosophypages.com/hy/2g.htm

Greece and the Psyche

tripartite soul: wisdom in the rational part, courage in the spiritual part and moderation in the appetitive. With wisdom in leadership, courage in its defense and moderation in all things, the state would flourish.

What Plato learned in practical life, of course, was that leaders sought power and lacked wisdom, warriors sometimes betrayed the state and the citizenry lacked moderation most of the time. We might conclude from this failure that his idea of the tripartite soul had the same fate. The story above of the warrior awakened from death would seem to suggest such a fate for the soul released from the bonds of life. For every wrong against another, the soul languished a hundred years and the punishment was extended for thousands of years for many wrongs committed.

This familiar scenario of paradise for the good and punishment for the wicked has its familiar account in the Christian allegory of heaven and hell. Indeed, Plato's treatment of the soul would have grater acceptance by both Judaism and Christianity had he not referred to divinity as The Good, rather than God. But he had to distinguish between the one God and the Olympians.

Finally, from the philosophers of this period in Greece, a word from Aristotle, whose thought ushered in materialism, the attention to and belief in what the senses were willing just barely able to tell us about the nature of the universe. Cut loose from the Academy, Aristotle was free to explore the world, to begin cataloging and collecting, making him the first museum curator. When confronted with the idea of a soul, Aristotle basically demurred. He described the psyche or soul as the essence of any living thing, and that it was not a substance distinct from the body.

In his thought, the soul was the essence that gave life to any and every living thing, plant or animal. In addition, it is the soul that gives its living host the characteristics natural to that entity. Therefore, the plant has a nutritive soul, the animal a sensitive soul and the human being a rational soul. For example, the animals ability to seek out food and avoid predators was a function of its soul, or basic nature. Finally, he believed that although the soul was not material but rather an essence in the body, it did not survive the death of the material body.

Aside from and yet alongside the work and teachings of philosophy in Athens during this period was the thousand year tradition of the Eleusinian Mysteries, an annual event of initiation which sometimes involved upwards of five thousand persons. This is not the space to describe the details of the how the mysteries were performed in Athens and Eleusis, where the major rituals took place, but a note on the relation of the initiation to the soul is to the purpose.

The famous myth of Demeter-Persephone is related to these new Classical ideas about the soul in that the Mysteries, which grew out of the myth, were intended to be the initiation of the individual soul into the brotherhood of the saved. The principle was transmitted through ceremony that the soul struggled just as the individual did to deal with its earthly and divine situation. It sought release through the perfection of its divine attributes, striving for rhythm and harmony with the gods.

Although the myth has agricultural connections and can be read at this simple level and also has psychological connections which can be applied to physical and mental existence, the most important interpretations have to do with spiritual transformation and consciousness. There are certain themes which have become associated with the Eleusinian Mysteries and its Homeric myth which appear again and again in the history and conduct of the rites. The first is the marriage of the Olympian sky gods to the gods of the underworld, or the marriage of conscious and subconscious forces and the resulting containment and transformation of the latter. Demeter is the Olympian spirit of the earth, a force of conscious spiritual power. Hades is an underworld god, king of the dead, keeper of souls, a symbol of subconscious power, but still a spiritual force as brother to Zeus. Persephone is the innocent maiden abducted to the underworld against her will. She is a savior for mankind, queen with Hades and yet virgin (pure spirit) on Olympus where she lives eight months of the year with her mother. Her return is the affirmation of immortality possible in the purified soul of human aspiration.

Because so many Greeks took part in this ritual and were given this secret knowledge and because the Eleusinian tradition lasted up to and even after Rome conquered Greece and Christianity became the official religion of the empire, the vision of the soul became woven into the new religion and as we shall see influenced the Church's position on the soul and its destiny, the topic of our next chapter.

CHAPTER 5

Christianity and the Soul

THE HISTORY OF the Early Christian Church from the death and resurrection of Jesus Christ to at least the early Fourth Century is shrouded in mythology, heresies and doctrinal debate. When I use the term shroud, I allude to the famous Shroud of Turin, thought to be the burial cloth of Jesus, but proven a cloth from the Renaissance, at least by the judgments of modern science, but still cherished by the faithful.

Even more shrouded is the history of the soul in this period, and we find that how this important attribute of religious belief was discussed was the province of philosophers and theologians, with the Church Fathers taking a secondary role as they struggled to establish Church structure and a religion for the people.

In the estimate of most objective historians, the most accurate history of that initial struggle is provided by the writings of St. Paul (3-67 BCE), his conversion testimony notwithstanding. Paul was a Jewish scholar (Saul of Tarsus) and by general agreement the greatest of the interpreters of the life of Jesus. His letters to the early churches in Corinth, Ephesus, Colossae, and Thessalonika illustrate the early trials of forming a religious tradition around the death and story of the resurrection of Jesus. To be learned and practiced were the communion ritual of the Last Supper, the procedures of the mass, the doctrines of redemption and the life of the priesthood. To come would be the establishment of the hierarchy, the naming of bishops and policies in regard to the Romans and Jews.

It was this last concern that most dominated the early Church. Small bands of Christians were holding to the doctrine of the end of the world coming soon, a doctrine most disturbing to the Romans in particular, who were busy maintaining the empire and dealing with barbarians at the gates. It is not surprising then that the early emperors tended to regard Christians as threats to the peace, progress and prosperity of Roman culture and survival.

As a result of this ragged beginning, it was not until the early fourth Century that the Church finally found acceptance and gained devoted followers. The date generally given for this change in fortune is 311 CE, with the death of Emperor Galerius, who was the last emperor to actively persecute Christians.

While all this difficulty was confronting the early churches we know from Paul, the philosophers and theologians were arguing about doctrines to be accepted, debated and rejected. Of these the issue of reincarnation continued to be discussed and debated in earnest, particularly in Alexandria, where the Hermetic movement and Gnosticism held center stage. And in the years after those who knew Jesus and the gospel writers of later years then came the next generation of Christians, those we call the Early Church Fathers.

Men such as Justin Martyr (AD 100–165), St. Clement of Alexandria (AD 150–220), and Origen (AD 185–254) taught in the years of early Church struggles and part of their teaching included reincarnation. For example, in his major work, "Against Celsus" Origen asked if it wasn't quite natural for a soul to be born into an embodiment based on a previous life's merits. He also stated, more clearly, that a soul had no beginning nor end.

St. Jerome (AD 340–420), translator of the Latin version of the Bible known as the Vulgate, in his Letter to Demetrias (a Roman matron), states that some Christian sects in his day taught a form of reincarnation as an esoteric doctrine, imparting it to a few "as a traditional truth which was not to be divulged." As a result that aspect of the life of the soul was set aside as not compatible with the gospels and teaching of Paul.

It was, then, at the Council of Nicea in 325 that the Bishops formulated the most important and lasting profession of faith in Church history: The Nicene Creed. A statement that was not just a profession of faith, it was also a story to be acknowledged and preserved for all time, one that is still spoken in churches of many, but not all Christian denominations in the world today. And the Creed is also critical to our understanding of the definition and destiny of the soul.

Here, then, as a starting point for our exploration, is the original text:

The Nicene Creen
We believe (I believe) in one God, the Father Almighty, maker of heaven and earth, and of all things visible and invisible. And in one Lord Jesus Christ, the only begotten Son of God, and born of the Father before all ages. (God of God) light of light, true God of true God. Begotten not made, consubstantial to the Father, by whom all things were made. Who for us men and for our salvation came down from heaven. And was incarnate of the Holy Ghost and of the Virgin Mary and was made

Christianity and the Soul

man; was crucified also for us under Pontius Pilate, suffered and was buried; and the third day rose again according to the Scriptures. And ascended into heaven, sits at the right hand of the Father, and shall come again with glory to judge the living and the dead, of whose Kingdom there shall be no end. And (I believe) in the Holy Ghost, the Lord and Giver of life, who proceeds from the Father (and the Son), who together with the Father and the Son is to be adored and glorified, who spoke by the Prophets. And one holy, catholic, and apostolic Church. We confess (I confess) one baptism for the remission of sins. And we look for (I look for) the resurrection of the dead and the life of the world to come. Amen."

The first thing we notice, if we are looking for some clarity about the destiny of the soul of ordinary people, is that nothing appears directly to the point. But, if we look closely, we find principles of faith that influence later positions.

First, the Church declared that Jesus was "consubstantial" with the father, meaning of the same substance and essence as God, making Jesus divine, who was made man and came to the Earth. Next, we see that He was crucified "also for us," which is a critically important phrase because it establishes the sacrifice made by Christ for our original sins. As a side note, I recall that for many years, as I walked to work each day, I passed a Baptist church which had a permanent sign in large type that said, "Christ died for your sins. What have you done for Him lately?" Guilt, of course, was the desired reaction. Finally, after our confession for the remission of our sins, we may look forward to the resurrection of the body (and presumably the soul as well) in the "world to come."

From that declaration on, and right up to today, the debate and punishments for heresy were essentially based on the notion of the interpretation of the word consubstantial. Was (is) Jesus Christ divine, or is he part human and partly divine, or was he a human being, a great soul gifted with wisdom, even divine knowledge of the truth? These questions were debated heatedly in the centuries after the Council of Nicea, especially in subsequent councils, such as the Council of Ephesus in 430 C.E. It was at his week long gathering of bishops from Rome, Constantinople and Alexandria that argued the issue of the divinity of Christ.

The major conflict took place between the bishops of Rome and Alexandria against the views of Nestorius, the Bishop of Constantinople, who took issue with the principle of consubstantiality. Nestorius taught that Jesus was part human and part divine. After all the debate the bishops, with the support of Pope St. Celestine, agreed on the following sentence"

The holy synod said: "Since in addition to the rest the most impious Nestorius has neither been willing to obey our citation, nor to receive the most holy and god-fearing bishops whom we sent to him, we have necessarily betaken ourselves to the examination of his impieties; and, having apprehended from his letters and from his writings, and from his recent sayings in this metropolis which have been reported, that his opinions and teachings are impious, we being necessarily impelled thereto both by the canons [for his contumacy] and by the letter [to Cyril] of our most holy father and colleague Celestine, Bishop of the Roman Church, with many tears have arrived at the following grievous sentence against him: Our Lord, Jesus Christ, Who has been blasphemed by him, has defined by this holy synod that

> *the same Nestorius is excluded from all episcopal dignity and from every assembly of bishops.*

The result, history tells us, was the first major schism in the Church between East and West, with the Eastern Church, usually named the Greek Orthodox, centered in Constantinople, and if we understand the Greek past and traditions, it is easy to see where lay the controversy.

As said earlier, this history is relevant to the destiny of the soul within Christianity because of these debates and heresies, the most important being the affirmation of the individual soul as part of the body, which at the Day of Judgment would be welcomed to life in the world to come. That said, history also proclaims clearly that the debate about the nature of the soul was to continue unabated, although not openly within the Church and its Nicene Creed. As we shall see later, another tradition, the sleeping soul, would also enter the debate and is still not resolved.

That said, it is also evident that the general debate about the nature of the soul became limited and simplified as the Church desired to teach a straightforward message to believers about immortality, heaven and hell. If we wish to locate a basic statement in this vein, we can look at this from Origen (185-254). He wrote:

> *The soul, having a substance and life of its own, shall after its departure from the world, be rewarded according to its deserts, being destined to obtain either an inheritance of eternal life and blessedness, if its actions shall have procured this for it, or to be delivered up to eternal fire and punishments, if the guilt of its crimes shall have brought it down to this...*

Thus the theme of reincarnation nearly disappeared with the general belief that souls were individual and connected eternally to the mind and body. Exceptions were rare. For example, Synesius (AD 370-480), Bishop of Ptolemais, also taught the concept of reincarnation, and in an ambiguous prayer that has survived, he says: "Father, grant that my soul may merge into the light, and be no more thrust back into the illusion of earth." Others of his Hymns, such as number III, contain lines clearly stating his views, and also pleas that he may be so purified that rebirth on earth will no longer be necessary. In a thesis on dreams, Synesius writes: "It is possible by labor and time, and a transition into other lives, for the imaginative soul to emerge from this dark abode." This passage reminds us of verses in the Revelation of John (3:12), with its symbolic, initiatory language leading into: "Him that overcometh will I make a pillar in the temple of my God, and he shall go no more out."

What is most interesting in this time of the end of pagan philosophy and the birth of the Christian era, is the struggle between worlds in thinkers like Oregin and Augustine, both students of Plato and also strongly moved by the life, death and resurrection of Jesus. Following Oregin, Augustine (354-430) addressed the immortality of the soul and its existence following the death of the body. He wrote that following the destruction of the body, the soul, still conscious because of its connection to mind, would live either with God or an isolated state of separation from God.

What is also interesting, philosophy aside for a moment, is the way in which the soul is portrayed in the Bible, both Old and New. The Old Testament is essentially divided between the Torah, or first five books, the Histories, and the Prophets. The word soul, usually translated as *nephesh* in the Hebrew appears multiple times, we learn, in 94 verses along with other words such as life and body. Generally, the word spirit is *ruach*, thus making a distinction, but again, in the three sections the words soul and spirit are used differently.

In Genesis, for example, the word *nephesh* refers to 'creatures' created by God, thus souls as living, breathing animals and people. In the book of Numbers, we see that a dead body can also be a soul, but not "have" a soul. This distinction is important and leads to the conclusion that in the Old Testament, 'nephesh' does not mean an immortal soul. When we move to the Histories the same usage applies. A *nephesh* is a person, both Hebrew and otherwise. Also, if a trap is laid to catch an animal, it is the soul that is caught.

The word 'spirit,' generally *ruach*, appears in twenty-seven verses, and is used in the sense of the spirit of life, as in God breathing into Adam's nose the breath of life. And in an important verse, we see in Psalm thirty-one "Into thine hand I commit my spirit (*ruach*): thou hast redeemed me, O LORD God of truth". When the Greeks translated the Old Testament, the word used was *pneuma*, or breath, again to make a distinction from spirit, which in the Greek would be *daimon*.

In the New Testament, the word soul is *psyche* in the Greek and the meaning is much the same, which we would expect from these Jewish writers. The word soul is used to designate life, which in the case of Jesus is given up for us. But the meaning is again life, rather than a distinctive immortal soul. In fact, nowhere in the Bible, old or new, is the word soul used overtly to designate an immortal soul.

What, then, are we to make of this usage, or lack of? Where does the notion in Christianity of an immortal soul arise if not in the Bible? What is striking is that immortality, at least in the

New Testament, will come only in the Day of Judgement. We see this in Luke:

> *Assuredly, I say to you, there is no one who has left house or parents or brothers or wife or children, for the sake of the kingdom of God, who shall not receive many times more in this present time, and in the age to come everlasting life* (Luke 18:29-30).

We shall have to wait, we are told, for the day of judgment to arise in body and spirit. And more clearly, Paul speaks more about immortality in Corinthians:

> *Behold, I tell you a mystery: We shall not all sleep, but we shall all be changed in a moment, in the twinkling of an eye, at the last trumpet. For the trumpet will sound, and the dead will be raised incorruptible, and we shall be changed. For this corruptible must put on incorruption, and this mortal must put on immortality. So when this corruptible has put on incorruption, and this mortal has put on immortality, then shall be brought to pass the saying that is written: "Death is swallowed up in victory."* (1st Corinthians 15:51-54).

It is Jesus only who possesses immortality, or an immortal soul. Finally, there are three more instances where the notion of immortality arises in the New Testament:

> *…who "will render to each one according to his deeds": eternal life to those who by patient continuance in doing good seek for glory, honor, and immortality* (Romans 2:6-7).

...our Savior Jesus Christ, who has abolished death and brought life and immortality to light through the gospel (2nd Timothy 1:10).

However, for this reason I obtained mercy, that in me first Jesus Christ might show all long suffering, as a pattern to those who are going to believe on Him for everlasting life. Now to the King eternal, immortal (1st Timothy 1:16-17).

What is generally the case following the spread of the Christian doctrines of the soul is that immortality is the province of the risen Christ, a doctrine which of course makes conversion to the faith a compelling option, whereas no other religion but the Eastern traditions offer either reincarnation or an indwelling immortal soul as a matter of course or in the nature of things.

It was not until after the end of formal pagan worship with the tragic death in 415 of Hypatia, the gifted pagan philosopher in Alexandria that Christian and pagan philosophies began to merge and become open for debate outside the reach of the Church in Rome. Hypatia was killed by a Christian mob because she would not publicly convert to the new faith. Her position and reputation made her refusal an affront to the new religion, and also being a woman she was vulnerable. Hypatia was a Neoplatonist and held the views of Plato and Plotinus, the latter who studied under Ammonius Saccus in Egypt in a tradition where the soul had immortal nature.

The powerful influence of Saccas on thinkers such as Plotinus, who studied with him before moving to Rome and also on Hypatia, who remained at the what was left of the great library in Alexandria, were just two of the many students who remained loyal to philosophy and who resisted the claims of the Church. Here, as an example, is an excerpt from Theosophic sources on the impact of this teaching:

> *The School of Ammonius Saccas was divided into two sections: exoteric and esoteric. This was merely the continuation of an ancient custom, for all the religious and philosophical schools of the past were divided in the same manner. The Mysteries of every nation consisted of the "lesser" and the "greater." The "lesser" mysteries were given to the public and consisted mainly in ethical teachings. The "greater" mysteries were reserved for the few. All of the great Adepts of olden times gave out their secret teachings only to those who had pledged themselves to silence. Even the Jews had their Mercavah, or outer vehicle, which concealed their highest knowledge. Northern Buddhism has its "greater" and "lesser" vehicle, known as the Mahayana, or esoteric, and Hinayana, or exoteric School. Pythagoras called his Gnosis "the knowledge of things that are", and revealed it only to his pledged disciples. Jesus spoke to the multitudes in parables and kept his secret teachings for the few. Therefore Ammonius, in dividing his own School into two sections, was following the lines of his predecessors.*

> *The Alexandrian Theosophists were divided into three classes: neophytes, initiates and masters. Their Rules were copied from those which had been used in the ancient Mysteries of Orpheus, who, according to Herodotus, had brought them from India. These Rules had come down to the Neoplatonists as their natural inheritance: "What Orpheus delivered in hidden allegories, Pythagoras learned when he was initiated into the Orphic*

Mysteries, and Plato next received a perfect knowledge of them from Orphic and Pythagorean writings."[13]

The Rules of Orpheus have again descended as a natural inheritance to the Theosophists of the present day. For Orpheus is no other than Arjuna, the disciple of Krishna who went around the world teaching the ancient Wisdom-Religion and establishing the Mysteries. Every time the modern Theosophist reads the Bhagavad-Gita he is acquainting himself with the ancient Orphic discipline. The system of Orpheus is one of the strictest morality, and the Orphic concept of duty one of the noblest known to mankind. The philosophical ideas of Orpheus are known to every student of The Secret Doctrine. In the Orphic system, the divine Essence is inseparable from whatever is in the manifested universe, all forms being concealed from all eternity in it. At determined periods these forms are manifested through the process known as Emanation. All things having proceeded from this divine Essence, all things must of necessity return to it. Innumerable transmigrations or reincarnations and purifications are needed before this final consummation can take place.

The philosophical system of Orpheus was revived in Egypt by Ammonius Saccas. The central idea of the Eclectic Theosophy was that of a single Supreme Essence, Unknown and Unknowable. The system was characterized by three distinct features: first, the theory of this Supreme Essence; second, the doctrine of the human soul, called an emanation of the Supreme Essence and therefore considered to be of the same nature; third, Theurgy, the art of using the divine powers of man to rule the blind forces of nature.

---

13 Alexander Wilder, *Neoplatonism and Alchemy*

The Soul's Journey

> *The aim and purpose of Ammonius was to reconcile all sects, peoples and nations under one common faith -- a belief in one Supreme Eternal Unknown and Unnamed Power which governs the universe by immutable and eternal laws. His object was to prove a primitive system of Theosophy, which in the beginning was known alike in all countries; to induce men to lay aside their quarrels and strifes and unite in purpose and thought as the children of one common mother; to purify the ancient religions, now corrupted and obscured, from all dross of human element by expounding their philosophical principles. His chief object was to extract from the various religious teachings, as from a many-stringed instrument, one full and harmonious chord which would find response in every truth-loving heart.*[14]

As we shall see, the teaching of Saccas and others of his persuasion has come down to us as the Perennial Philosophy. By contrast, what we have seen in this chapter on the Early Church is the beginning of a religion and of an historic power struggle to make Christianity the world's faith. The doctrine of a future immortality was crucial for the recruitment of followers, those without any previous sense of a soul within themselves. After all, philosophy is not a common pastime. It takes dedication, discipline, passion and time to attain the wisdom it teaches. Thinkers like Saccas, Plotinus and Hypatia, who remained outside the reaches of the Church in those early years, gave us the openness and freedom to explore our own nature outside the restraints of authority and that freedom is what allows us to respond even now when we find the strength to seek within for knowledge and understanding.

---

14 THEOSOPHY, Vol. 25, No. 2, December, 1936

Christianity and the Soul

Next, we explore how the visionary company of the Neoplatonists took the philosophy of Plato and his references to the soul and with that encouragement developed a dramatically different approach in opposition to early Christian doctrine. What emerged as a result influenced later thought, culminating in the coming conflicts during the Italian Renaissance and Reformation.

CHAPTER 6

Neoplatonism and Christianity

HISTORIANS OF PHILOSOPHY and religion generally agree that Neoplatonism was a significant influence on Christianity and not the other way around. What we learned in the last chapter about the position of the early Church on the soul in the light of the Day of Judgment and the End Times changed significantly as time went on and it became evident that the end of the world was not immanent.

In particular, the works of Plotinus on the One and the immortal soul influenced later Christian doctrine. As a result of Plotinus, there was a "loosening" of dogma on the soul to the point that all human beings possessed this divine emanation from the Logos or One into our nature, at least in some church doctrinal statements. The shift was not an easy one for the Church, but the argument from Plotinus was so persuasive that to ignore his rational arguments was impossible.

What follows are excerpts from a dialogue between Plotinus and Porphyry when the two met for the first time. Note the progression of the thesis on soul. We begin with comments on the One or Absolute.

PORPHYRY: "Must I then conclude that this Principle, being above all, is not to be perceived in the manifested universe? Where is the One?"

PLOTINUS: "The One is everywhere. There is no space where It is not. Therefore It fills everything. It is by the One that everything exists. The One fills everything, and produces everything, without being that which It produces."

PORPHYRY: "But, Plotinus, thou knowest as well as I that the whole manifested universe is characterized by motion! Is Motion the One? Or is the potentiality of Motion a condition of rest? What is the relation of the One to rest and motion?"

PLOTINUS: "The One is superior to both rest and motion. It is the potentiality of both rest and motion, and consequently it is superior to both."

PORPHYRY: "Another thought occurs to me, great Teacher. The universe manifests intelligence. Can that which thou describest as the One be Intelligence itself? In other words, does the One think?"

PLOTINUS: "The One does not think, because it comprises both the thinker and the thought. The One is not Intelligence, but is superior to Intelligence. As it is superior to Intelligence, that which emanates must of necessity be intelligence."

PORPHYRY: "This Principle which underlies thy philosophy is indeed profound. I clearly see that the One transcends the power of human conception. Wilt thou not bring me down into regions which can be comprehended by my finite mind? What follows this condition of potentiality? How does the manifested universe come into existence?"

PLOTINUS: "Everything that exists after the One is derived from the One. But this second stage is no longer the ONE, but the multiple One. We see that all things that reach perfection cannot remain in an unmanifest condition, but must produce themselves in manifestation. This is seen throughout the whole of nature. Not only are beings capable of choice, but even those lacking in soul perception have a tendency to impart to other beings what is in them. As, for instance, fire emits heat; snow emits cold. Therefore all things in nature seek to reach immortality by the manifestation of their qualities. The One manifests Itself. That which is manifested also manifests itself in its own way."

PORPHYRY: "Ah, I see! Thou teachest the Doctrine of Emanations as the Gnostics do! But thou forgettest, Plotinus, that manifested things are made of matter. How can matter manifest itself?"

PLOTINUS: "Matter is not dead. Matter is not devoid of life or intelligence. One cannot exist without the other. Reciprocally, intelligible entities do not exist without the matter that makes them. Form and matter are principles that are necessary to the constitution of all things."

[Now, at this point, Porphyry has elicited from Plotinus the fundamental structure of emanations and the workings of the One in relation to the other human attributes of spirit and consciousness. He is now ready to ask what other quality of attribute do human beings possess that connects them to the One. The dialogue continues]

PORPHYRY: "I See, Plotinus. Thy theory is that Spirit, or Consciousness, and Matter are not to be regarded as independent realities, but as the two facets, or aspects, of the One, which constitute the basis of conditioned being, whether subjective or objective. But what about man? Is there something in man that corresponds to the One?"

PLOTINUS: "There must be another nature, different from the body, which possesses existence from itself. It is necessary that there should be a certain nature primarily vital, which is also necessarily indestructible and immortal, as being the Principle of Life to other things. It is necessary that there should be something which is the supplier of life, the supplier being external to, and beyond corporeal nature."

PORPHYRY: "Is that what men call the Soul? If so, what is the relation of the Soul to the One?"

PLOTINUS: "Soul is One, and in a certain respect the ONE. The soul which has more alliance with the One participates more abundantly in It."

PORPHYRY: "What is the nature of the Soul?"

> PLOTINUS: "The Soul is not corporeal, as the Stoics taught. No aggregation of atoms could produce the Soul. The Soul is an incorporeal and immortal essence. The Soul imparts movement to everything else. She imparts life to the body. She alone possesses real life."

[At this point, Plotinus has established the fundamental nature of the soul, giving it a feminine nature, which is also in Greek tradition the nature of wisdom. He connects soul to god – the One– directly, without using the Greek term *theos*, for god. Plotinus wants to stay away from a creator god in the tradition of the Gnostics, and yet he does not establish the One as the same as Being, which in Parmenides is more abstract. The issue here, however, is soul and it is clear that Plotinus sees soul as the fundamental essence of the human being. We are soul in a temporary body. Plotinus thought the body a nuisance, even an aberration, an attitude which historically made him less attractive to later thinkers, but in the matter of the soul, he was taken very seriously, and as we shall see, as even in Renaissance Italy, believers in the immortal soul were not convicted of heresy by the Inquisition. The next sequence introduces the principle of the World Soul.]

> PORPHYRY: "What in thy opinion, is the relation of all Souls with the Universal World-Soul?"

> PLOTINUS: "The Universe lies in the Soul that sustains it, and no part is destitute of Soul, being moistened with life like a net in water. If all souls be one in the Universal World-Soul, why should they not together form One? If

both my soul and your soul proceed from the Universal World-Soul, then all Souls form but a single One."

PORPHYRY: "How then, Plotinus, wouldst thou define man? Is he fundamentally a Soul or does he only possess a Soul?"

PLOTINUS: "Man is a Soul. He has a body. The nature and essence of these must be divided. Since the body is a composite, reason shows that it cannot remain perpetually the same. Sense likewise shows that it is dissolved at death and receives various destructions, since each of the things inherent in it tends to its own, or to the whole from which it was derived. Soul is separable from the body. Nor yet is the soul in the body, as part of the whole. For soul is not a part of the body."

PORPHYRY: "But is the body not a part of us, Plotinus?"

PLOTINUS: "If the body is a part of us, we are not wholly immortal. But when we see correctly, we see that the body is only the instrument of the soul, and that the soul is the man himself."

PORPHYRY: "But, Plotinus, even though the body is only the instrument of the soul, it is an important one. We could not function without it!"

PLOTINUS: "We are not the body, but we are not entirely separated from it. It is associated with us. It depends upon us. Therefore its sufferings and pleasures are not indifferent to us. The weaker we are, the more we occupy

The Soul's Journey

ourselves with it. In it is plunged a part of ourselves, which constitutes the essential personality."

PORPHYRY: "Why then, Plotinus, do men speak of the soul as if it were the body?"

PLOTINUS: "The soul is said to be in the body because the body alone is visible. But if we could see the soul, and if we could see that she surrounds the body by the life she possesses, we would say that the soul is in no way in the body, but that on the contrary the body is the contained within the container, that which flows within the immovable."

PORPHYRY: "Wouldst thou give an illustration, Plotinus, so that the matter will be clearer to my comprehension?"

PLOTINUS: "The soul is said to be in the body as a pilot in a ship. If it were there as a passenger, it would be there only by accident. But even this is not enough. For the pilot is not present in the whole of the ship, but only in a part of it at one time, while the soul is always present everywhere. A better illustration is that the soul is present in the body as light is present in air. Light is present in air without mingling with it. When the air, within which the light radiates, withdraws its light, the air keeps none of the light. But it is illuminated as long as the air remains subject to the light."

PORPHYRY: "I thank thee, Plotinus, for thy illustrations. But there is another question I would like to ask thee. Thou saidst a few moments ago that a part of ourselves is plunged in the body. Must I understand that the whole soul is not present in the body?"

PLOTINUS: "The soul never enters completely into the body. By her higher part, she ever remains united to the intelligible world, as by her lower part she remains united to the sense world. The higher part of the soul is insensible to the attraction of these transitory pleasures and leads an undisturbed life. Every soul has a lower part turned toward the body, and a higher part turned toward the divine intelligence."

PORPHYRY: "Ah, I see! The nature of the soul becomes dual as soon as it is attached to a body! That would necessarily give it a double action!"

PLOTINUS: "Exactly! The soul has a double action in her double relation to what is above and what is below. By her first action, she manages the body, and by her second action she contemplates the intelligible entities."

PORPHYRY: "I understand. The soul is therefore an active entity. What are some of her activities?"

PLOTINUS: "The soul is a real being, with characteristic nature and activities. Among these is memory, whose exercise is only hindered by the body. When the soul unites with the body, she forgets. When she separates herself from the body, she remembers. The body is therefore only the stream of Lethe, or forgetfulness. To the soul alone belongs memory."

PORPHYRY: "Thou hast said that the soul is the man himself. How can we arrive at this conclusion?"

PLOTINUS: "Consider the soul by taking away that which is extraneous. Or rather, let him who takes this away survey himself, and he will see himself as immortal when he beholds himself in the intelligible world, and situated in a pure abode. For he will perceive himself as intellect surveying not anything sensible, but an eternal power contemplating that which is eternal."

PORPHYRY: "How then does the soul acquire a body? Is there a Law which causes her to incarnate in a body of flesh?"

PLOTINUS: "What is called inevitable necessity and divine justice consists in the sway of nature which causes each soul to proceed in an orderly manner into the bodily image which has become the object of her affection. Consequently the soul approaches the object toward which her interior disposition bears her. Thus she is led and introduced where she is to go. At a fixed moment she descends, as it were, spontaneously, where she ought to enter. Each soul has her own hour. When this hour arrives, the soul descends as if a herald had called her. Thus individuals come here below by virtue of the common law to which they are subjected."

PORPHYRY: "Ah, Plotinus, it seems that thou teachest of a power outside of man! The Law of which thou speakest, where is it? From whom is it derived?"

PLOTINUS: "Each one bears within himself this common Law, a Law which does not derive its power from outside, but which depends upon the nature of those who are subject to it, because it is innate in them."

PORPHYRY: "What purpose, then, has the soul in incarnating?"

PLOTINUS: "The soul descends for the purpose of developing her own powers, and to adorn what is below her. Souls alternately changing their bodies pass to other forms, just as in the scenes of a play, where one of the actors apparently dies, but shortly after changes his dress, and, assuming the appearance of another person, returns to the scene."

PORPHYRY: "What then, Plotinus, is death?"

PLOTINUS: "To die is only to change body, no otherwise than shifting a garment. Nevertheless he who departs will hereafter return to the play."

[Plotinus here affirms the role of reincarnation, where the soul possesses the memory of the particular lifetime before moving on the next. Here, he and the Church parted company, not accepting the role of the soul in being central to a pattern of lives. For the Church, if allowing the notion of an immortal soul to exist in every being, then that soul must enter into a state of purgatory, there to remain until the Judgment. Here is a description of the doctrine of purgatory

> *The Catechism of the Catholic Church defines purgatory as a "purification, so as to achieve the holiness necessary to enter the joy of heaven," which is experienced by those "who die in God's grace and friendship, but still imperfectly purified" (CCC 1030). It notes that "this final purification of the elect... is entirely different from the punishment of the damned" (CCC 1031).*
>
> *The purification is necessary because, as Scripture teaches, nothing unclean will enter the presence of God in heaven (Rev. 21:27) and, while we may die with our mortal sins forgiven, there can still be many impurities in us, specifically venial sins and the temporal punishment due to sins already forgiven.[15]*

The contrast between Plotinus and the Church could not be more dramatic. Plotinus tells us that after the death of a temporary body, the soul, which is our real identity, returns "to the play." This world, then, suffering notwithstanding, is the play. On the other hand, the church must create a place for the soul to go after death in order to wait for the final Judgment. This timeless place, Purgatory, was set aside by the Church as a convenience in the light of its decision to assign a soul to every person, and for those who are baptized, those souls are preserved. Those not baptized are lost. This state of affairs has been studied by the church, particularly where a baby dies before baptism. Here is the latest doctrine on the subject as reported by the Washington Post in 2007:

> *After three years of study, a Vatican-appointed panel of theologians has declared that limbo is a "problematic" concept that Catholics are free to reject. The 30-member International*

---

15 *"Catholic Answers"* IMPRIMATUR: *In accord with 1983 CIC 827*

> *Theological Commission said there are good reasons to believe instead that unbaptized babies go to heaven, because God is merciful and "wants all human beings to be saved."*

However, some Catholic conservatives do not agree with this reasoning. The article goes on:

> *"Some Catholics, however, are standing firm on limbo. "The Vatican is suggesting that salvation is possible without baptism. That is heresy," said Kenneth J. Wolfe, Washington columnist for the Remnant, a traditionalist Catholic newspaper. He predicted that the 41-page report, titled "The Hope of Salvation for Infants Who Die Without Being Baptized," would undermine the church's advice to parents to make sure that children are baptized within the first 10 days of life. It might also undercut the church's position against abortion, since 'one of the reasons for opposing abortion is that the baby's soul is lost,' he said."*

Although the Catholic Church still adheres to the related idea of purgatory -- a period of punishment and purification before the full joy of heaven -- it has been inching away from limbo for decades. Most Catholic schools gradually stopped teaching children about limbo in the 1960s, '70s and '80s, according to Monsignor Daniel Kutys, director of religious education for the U.S. Conference of Catholic Bishops.

This "reasoning" of course begs the question and is meant to pacify the grief of Church members who agonize over the fate of a deceased child. Plotinus, on the other hand, who loved children and taught them in his home had a much more humane answer in that the souls of all people after death just return "to the play" that is earthly existence.

This position is a recognition of the Neoplatonic tradition of emanation from above, in other words from the Good. Body, mind and soul emanate from the source and the soul, which has memory (Mind) returns and some people have a memory of these past incarnations, as we learn today from more open accounts from India.

The Catholic Church finds itself in a highly awkward position, mostly, as we see aboe, from the issue of abortion. Since the Church argues that the soul enters the body of the fetus at conception, an aborted fetus is eternally lost. Naturally, this is a powerful argument against abortion, whereas in the Eastern traditions, the soul enters the child much later, and in the event of an early death simply returns in another embodiment.

Presently, the Catholic Catechism contains the following acknowledgment of the presence of soul within:

The soul is the subject of human consciousness and freedom; soul and body together form one unique human nature. Each human soul is individual and immortal, immediately created by God. The soul does not die with the body, from which it is separated by death, and with which it will be reunited in the final resurrection.[16]

This introduction of the soul in the Church entered the doctrines in the 5th Century influenced by St Augustine. A study of the thinking of Augustine on the soul begins with his acceptance of the principles expressed by Plotinus. His "Treatise on the Soul"

---
16 *Index of the Roman Catholic Catechism*

Neoplatonism and Christianity

illustrates his effort to move gradually from Plotinus, whom he admired, to the Church orthodoxy he was serving. In later life, he discussed the notion of the fallen soul entering into the human body, there to be reconciled with God at some indefinite point.

What is unique and crucial to our study is that since Augustine and because of his theory of the fallen soul, human beings carry the guilt of Adam's disobedience in their soul and must be forgiven. We bear this guilt, the theory goes, within and must adhere to the teachings of the Church in order to attain salvation. It is this separation from the teachings of Plotinus that gave Christianity its particular distinction in the nature and character of the soul.

Because there is no further reference to a definition of the soul in the Catechism, the taint of the fallen soul remains. What is interesting for our study is that in order to establish the theory of the fallen soul, Augustine after the year 415 retained the original view of Plotinus that the soul preceded the birth of a new life and in the process of ensoulment shared the sin of Adam. It is interesting that there is no further explanation of the original source of the soul prior to embodiment.[17]

The lasting implication of these theories of soul in the Church is that those who follow Church doctrine are taught that human beings are fallen from the original sin of Adam and must seek forgiveness before entering heaven. This fallen soul, established in doctrine from Augustine onwards has been a point of contention in Christianity since that time.

In the next chapter we will see how another group of spiritual thinkers approached the life and nature of the soul without the taint of original sin.

---

17 Ronnie J. Rombs, *Saint Augustine and the Fall of the Soul*, pgs.74-86

CHAPTER 7

Hermes Elevates the Soul

AT THE SAME time that the Early Church was organizing itself as a powerful new religious force throughout the Mediterranean world, another small group of spiritual thinkers and seekers after the truth of reality were working in Alexandria with Neoplatonic philosophy, Egyptian symbolist philosophy, and early Christian developments to formulate a theory of soul, an effort which still influences philosophic and spiritual thought today.

Centered on the myths and teaching of Hermes Trismegistus, the thrice-blessed, these few sought to understand the soul and to form a tradition around its nature and potential for salvation and union with God. Hermeticism, as the sect was known, taught the principles of universal mind, the human being's connection to God, and the means by which the soul makes that connection.

In a dramatic contrast between the content of chapter six and the Early church, the Hermetists, as they were known, saw the universe and human life as an integral part of it as the effort and task to devote their lives to elevation, to raise the body, mind and soul to the level of the beauty of the universe.

As we learn from the Hermetic texts, first assembled and preserved for our study by Marcilio Ficino in the fifteenth Century in Florence, the teaching was based on the principles of three Great Planes of existence" the Physical, the Mental and the Spiritual.

Hermes Elevates the Soul

Although each of these planes have numerous sub-planes, the Great Planes formed the ground of teaching. Our interest, involving as it does the story of the waking soul, will be centered on the Spiritual Plane, even though it is the most difficult, the most challenging and the least understood of the planes. Here, for example, is a section of a text known as the Kybalion, an early 20th Century text on Hermeticism, to describe the Spiritual Plane:

Only the most advanced Hermetists are able to grasp the Inner Teachings regarding the state of existence, and the powers manifested on the Spiritual Planes. The phenomena is so much higher than that of the Mental Planes that a confusion of ideas would surely result from an attempt to describe the same. Only those whose minds have been carefully trained along the lines of the Hermetic Philosophy for years—yes, those who have brought with them from other incarnations the knowledge acquired previously—can comprehend just what is meant by the Teaching regarding these Spiritual Planes. And much of these Inner Teachings is held by the Hermetists as being too sacred, important and even dangerous for general public dissemination. The intelligent student may recognize what we mean by this when we state that the meaning of "Spirit" as used by the Hermetists is akin to "Living Power"; "Animated Force;" "Inner Essence;" "Essence of Life," etc., which meaning must not be confounded with that usually and commonly employed in connection with the term, i.e., "religious; ecclesiastical; spiritual; ethereal; holy," etc., etc. To occultists the word "Spirit" is used in the sense of "The Animating Principle," carrying with it the idea of Power, Living

The Soul's Journey

Energy, Mystic Force, etc. And occultists know that that which is known to them as "Spiritual Power" may be employed for evil as well as good ends (in accordance with the Principle of Polarity), a fact which has been recognized by the majority of religions in their conceptions of Satan, Beelzebub, the Devil, Lucifer, Fallen Angels, etc. And so the knowledge regarding these Planes has been kept in the Holy of Holies in all Esoteric Fraternities and Occult Orders,—in the Secret Chamber of the Temple.[18]

As this text illustrates, Hermeticism has an element of esotericism and deep mystery as part of its study and practice, but for our purpose, it is the movement of the soul in the Great Spiritual Plane that engages us.

In the study of Hermeticism, one of the principles that helps us to understand how the soul is capable of elevation is the Law of Correspondence, where the saying, "As above, so below" tells us that as the nature of things in the Spiritual realm holds true, so too is the case in the Physical and Mental planes. This principle is essentially Neoplatonic as Plotinus expressed the same idea in his theory of emanations, where the spiritual realm emanates its nature down to the earthly planes.

If we reverse the idea, then the state of things below can also reach up to the planes above as well. The human soul, then, can achieve near divine status through work on the Spiritual Plane. We will see this pattern in the teaching contained in the Hermetic dialogues as presented in the text *The Way of Hermes*.

---

18   *Three Initiates (2011-03-23). The Kybalion A Study of The Hermetic Philosophy of Ancient Egypt and Greece* (pp. 133-134). Kindle Edition.

Book 1

Poimandres to Hermes Trismegistus

1. Once, when mind had become intent on the things which are, and my understanding was raised to a great height, while my bodily senses were withdrawn as in sleep, when men are weighed down by too much food or by the fatigue of the body, it seemed that someone immensely great of infinite dimensions happened to call my name and said to me:

   'What do you wish to hear and behold, and having beheld what do you wish to learn and know?'

2. 'Who are you?' said I.

   He said, 'I am Poimandres the *Nous* (Mind) of the Supreme. I know what you wish and I am with you everywhere.'

3. 'I wish to learn,' said I, 'the things that are and understand their nature and to know God. O how I wish to hear these things!'

   He spoke to me again. 'Hold in your Mind all that you wish to learn and I will teach you.'....

5. Out of the light came forth the Holy Word which entered into the watery substance, and pure fire leapt from the watery substance and rose up; the fire was insubstantial, piercing and active. The air, being light, followed the breath, and mounted up till it reached the fire, away from earth and water, so that it seemed to be suspended from the fire. The earth and water remained in their own place mingled together, so that they could not be distinguished,

The Soul's Journey

and they were kept in motion by the breath of the Word, which passed over them within hearing.

6. Poimandres spoke to me and said:

    'Have you understood what you have seen and what it means?' 'I shall come to know it,' I said.

    'That light,' he said, 'is I, *Nous*, your God, who was before the watery substance which appeared out of the darkness; and the clear Word from *Nous* is the Son of God.'

    'How can this be?' said I.

    'Know this,' he said. 'That which sees and hears within you is the Word of the Lord, and Mind is God the Father. They are not separate from each other, for their union is life.'

    'Thank you,' I said.

    'But perceive the light and know it,' said Poimandres.

7. And when he had thus spoken, he looked at me full in the face for a long time, so that his form made me tremble. When he had looked up, I saw in my own *Nous* that the light was in innumerable powers, having become an infinite world. I saw a fire encompassed by a mighty power, being under command to keep its place; I was intent upon these things, seeing them by means of the word of Poimandres.

8. As I stood amazed, Poimandres spoke again to me, saying:

    You saw in Mind the first form, which is prior to the beginning of the beginingless and endless.' Thus spoke Poimandres to me.

    'Then,' I said, 'whence did the elements of nature have their origins?'

He answered: 'From the will of God, which, holding the Word and seeing the beautiful cosmos made one exactly like it, fashioned from her own constituent elements and the offspring of souls.[19]

First, Poimandres is the name given to the Mind of God in this teaching, and in Book 1 the student is nameless, but in Book 2 the student is Asclepius and the teacher is Hermes. What we see at first glance is that the form of the teaching looks Platonic, although the dialogue is more of a direct teaching as opposed to the dialectic used by Socrates. The dialogue format here allows us to participate and take the role of student.

Next, the teaching opens with a vision of the spiritual realm, which is an important step exhibited by the student, showing the teacher that he may be prepared to learn at this high level. The student has seen the beginning of eternity, the beginingless and endless. Then, when the student asks whence did the elements of nature have their origins, Mind answers that first it was from the will of God, then from the Logos, or Word, fashioning a cosmos from God's will in the same form as existed above, and, most important for our study, from the offspring of souls.

We then jump ahead to verse 25, which describes how the soul moves through stages to reach a spiritual realm where it can approach the divine. It should be noted that this journey does not begin from a fallen state but merely from the physical as the soul rises up through the harmony of the cosmos.

---

19 *The Way of Hermes*, Book, v. 1-8

25. 'Thus a man starts to rise up through the harmony of the cosmos. To the first plane he surrenders the activity of growth and diminution; to the second the means of evil, trickery now being inactive; to the third covetous deceit, now inactive, and to the fourth the eminence pertaining to a ruler, being now without avarice; to the fifth impious daring and reckless audacity and to the sixth evil impulses for wealth, all of these being now inactive, and to the seventh plain the falsehood which waits in ambush.
26. 'Then, stripped of the activities of the cosmos, he enters the substance of the eighth plane with his own power, and he sings praises to the Father with those who are present; those nearby who rejoice at his coming. Being made like to those who are there together, he also hears certain powers which are above the eighth sphere, singing praises to God with sweet voice. Then in due order, they ascend to the Father and they surrender themselves to the powers, and becoming the powers they are merged in God. This is the end, the Supreme Good, for those who have had the higher knowledge: to become God. Well then, why do you delay? Should you not, having received all, become the guide to those who are worthy, so that the human race may be saved by God through you?'
27. Having said that to me, Poimandres mingled with the powers. When I had thanked and praised the Father of the All, I was freed by him, having been strengthened and instructed in the nature of all and in the most high vision, and I began to proclaim to men the beauty of piety and knowledge:

O people, men born of the earth, who have given yourselves over to drink and sleep, and to ignorance of God, be sober, cease being intoxicated, cease being beguiled by dull sleep.'

28. Those who heard came to my side with one accord. I said: 'Why, O men born of earth, have you given yourselves over to death while having the power to partake of immortality? Repent. You who have kept company with those who have wandered and have shared in ignorance, be released from the dark light, take part in immortality. Put an end to destruction.'

29. Some of them kept on chattering and stood aloof, giving themselves over to the path of death; others begged to be instructed, having thrown themselves at my feet. Lifting them up, I became the guide of the race, teaching the words of God, how they could be saved. I sowed in them the words of wisdom and they were nourished by the water of immortality. As the evening came and the rays of the sun began fully to set, I bade them to thank God; when they had fully given thanks each returned to his own bed.

30. I engraved in myself the beneficent kindness of Poimandres and having been filled with what I desired, I was delighted. For the sleep of the body became the sobriety of the soul, the closing of the eyes became true vision, my silence became pregnant with the Supreme Good, and the utterance of the Word became the generation of riches. All this came to me who had received it from my *Nous*, that is to say from Poimandres, the Mind of the Supreme. I have come, divinely inspired by the truth. Wherefore, I give praise to God the Father with my whole soul and strength.

In verse 25 we see how the rising soul sheds the layers of physical existence, all natural in the course of things. We learn that this surrender takes place as a matter of course if the Mind has been opened and directed to the task of elevation. In verse 29, we see the course to follow and the peace it brings to one who wishes to know, having been "inspired by the truth."

In the remaining manuscripts of the Hermeticum are sixteen texts, of these are thirteen so-called books and three additional texts in the form of letters and a sermon. What follows now is not a comprehensive summary of these texts but rather an examination of the Hermetic doctrine on the soul: its nature, its function in the process of spiritual development, and its destiny. The translation we will use is the Mead translation, which is in the public domain. The Salaman et all translation from Inner Traditions is more contemporary in style but not any more illuminating than the older Mead.

In the Hermetic creation story we have this sequence:

> *Earth was as woman, her Water filled with longing; ripeness she took from Fire, spirit from Aether. Nature thus brought forth frames to suit the form of Man. And Man from Light and Life changed into soul and mind - from Life to soul, from Light to Mind.*

Soul then comes from Life, not the reverse. And Mind comes from Light. These words are capitalized, are operational forces in the hierarchy of Being. Therefore, if we cannot have soul without life, what does this say about the nature of soul? The implication is that soul is a refinement of the life force, a subtle energy which when activated and developed has the power to survive the more gross material manifestations of life. The implication may be that the manifestation of soul is not fundamental but rather a resultant effect of subtle refinement.

Also, when we look at the next line, we see a confirmation of that sense. "And thus continued all the sense-world's parts until the period of their end and new beginnings." The reference to new beginnings is the province of soul and its journey.

At the end of Book 1, we have the student's prayer of thanks and hope for greater knowledge and wisdom. He prays: "Accept my reason's offerings pure, from soul and heart for aye stretched up to Thee, O Thou unutterable, unspeakable, Whose Name naught but the Silence can express." His mind, through reason, prays for purity of thought, coming as it does from the fine energy of the soul and the passion of the heart, the seat of life itself.

The beginning of Book 3 speaks of the role of what Hermes calls "The Cyclic Gods," that is the powers that make and sustain all manner of creatures including human beings. Here is one expression of their work: "For every birth of flesh ensouled, and of the fruit of seed, and every handiwork, though it decay, shall of necessity renew itself, both by the renovation of the Gods and by the turning-round of Nature's rhythmic wheel." The reference to reincarnation as Nature's rhythmic wheel expresses the notion of repetition and return of the ensouled.

And at the close of Book 5 we see again the sequence of creation and where the soul fits the sequence. "For that the subtler part of matter is the air, of air the soul, of soul the mind, and of mind God." the soul is in its energy and substance more subtle than air and more subtle still is the mind and finally the mind of

The Soul's Journey

God. This pattern affirms the lack of physical measurement of the soul except as energy.

That fine energy of the wise is contrasted with what takes place among the ignorant, where the soul is weighed down by the heavy burden of ignorance. This reference from Book 7 makes the point in dramatic fashion: "For that the ill of ignorance doth pour o'er all the earth and overwhelm the soul that's battened down within the body, preventing it from fetching port within Salvation's harbors." The soul thus burdened down becomes the cargo that sinks the loaded vessel crossing the Mediterranean in a tempest of ignorance.

In the brief Book 8, Hermes himself is the teacher and Tat, who is young in this cosmic work, is the student. The book is entitled "On Soul and Body" and we would expect to find a clarification of how the embodied soul survives the mortal remains after death. The instruction here is, however, dense and unclear, except to argue that since God is immortal and has made man in his own image, then there is immortality in man.

Here are the key paragraphs:

And however much material there was, it being subject to His disposal, the Father turned it all into a body. He raised it up and made it spherical, conferring this quality on what He had wrought: namely an immortal and eternal materiality. When He had sown certain kinds of causal forms into the sphere, He enclosed them as within a cavern. As He wished to adorn the material within Himself with all qualities, He invested the whole body with immortality, so that this material would not wish itself separate from its composition with the body, and thus dissolve into its own undifferentiated state. When this material was not a body it was undifferentiated, my son. In this world other small things, such as growth and diminution, which men call death are enveloped by this material.

This undifferentiated state exists in respect of earthly beings. The bodies of the celestials have one order which was assigned to them by the Father in the beginning; and this indestructible order is kept unbroken by the periodic return of each body in the cosmic cycle. Within that cycle earthly bodies are formed, returned and dissolved into bodies that are indestructible, that is immortal. Thus there is deprivation of the senses but no destruction of bodies.

The third living being, man, has been begotten in the image of the cosmos, but, as the Father willed, not living like other earthly creatures. Not only does he have affinity with the second God, but also a conception of the first. He perceives the second God as a body, the first he conceives as without a body and as Nous, that is the Supreme Good.

Several confusing notions are presented here. The first is the reference to the Second God, which is a Gnostic thread, rejected by the Early Church and by history in general. Also, we find a reference to the celestial realm, the angelic world, also rejected by most but not all religious belief, and referenced here as part of the cosmic nature.

At the end of the explanation, we join Tat is seeking to clarify the teaching as he asks:

Tat:"Then does this being, man, not die?" And the answer is brusk:

Hermes: Hush, son! and understand what God, what Cosmos [is], what is a life that cannot die, and what a life subject to dissolution. Yea, understand the Cosmos is by God and in God; but Man by Cosmos and in Cosmos. The source and limit and the constitution of all things is God.

In Book 9, Hermes continues to sermonize, but in this case to Asclepius, who is an evolved seeker ready to be elevated to higher station in knowledge and wisdom. As a result, we hear Hermes being more direct and even intimate. What we encounter in the center of the book is this illuminating description of the spiritual realm in which we find ourselves:

For man is separated into soul and body, and only when the two sides of his sense agree together, does utterance of its thought conceived by mind take place. For it is mind that doth conceive all thoughts - good thoughts when it receives the seeds from God, their contraries when it receives them from the daimonials [spirits]; no part of Cosmos being free of daimon, who stealthily doth creep into the daimon who's illumined by God's light <i.e., the human soul>, and sow in him the seed of its own energy.

You may have noticed that the reference to God's Light, ie soul, is referenced here and picks up that image from the Hermetic creation story above. We can also reference the account in Genesis and say that when the command "Let there be light" was uttered, the substance of soul was also created and felt as energy. The connection between light and soul reflects the principle that with light and soul both created at the outset, where light occurred soul did as well.

Hermes Elevates the Soul

It is also clear from these references that God's spirit is different from soul and from the spirit world in general, and that as Hermes implies, daimon or spirit enters into the soul and the risk exists of a demonic spirit entering the soul as well as the Good. Thus in the next verse we have this:

And mind conceives the seed thus sown, adultery, murder, parricide, [and] sacrilege, impiety, [and] strangling, casting down precipices, and all such other deeds as are the work of evil daimons.

We are presented here with the concept of the pure versus the corrupted soul and in Book 10, this theme, in a dialogue again between Hermes and the young Tat, is given a full measure of attention. We look here in the modern translation, which is more direct and is clearer in its direction.

> *18. Whenever Mind is separated from its earthy body, it immediately puts on its own cloak of fire which it could not have in its earthy body, for earth cannot bear fire. It is all burnt up, even by a tiny spark. Therefore water is spread round the earth as a defense or a wall to hold off the flames of fire. Mind being faster than all divine thought and faster than all elements has fire as a body. Being the Creator of all, Nous uses fire as an instrument of his creative activity. The Universal Mind creates everything, the mind of man only earthly things. Stripped of fire Mind in man can create nothing divine, being human by reason of where it dwells.*
>
> *19. The human soul, that is not every human soul, but a pious one, is spiritual and divine. When such a soul has freed itself from the body and passed the test of piety, which is to know God and to harm no man, it becomes pure Mind. But the impious soul*

remains in its own substance, restricted by itself, seeking an earthy body, that is to say a human body into which it may enter. No other body has room for a human soul; and it is not lawful for a human soul to fall into the body of an irrational creature. It is the law of God to protect the human soul from such an outrage.

First, what we find in this text is Plato's definition of soul. It has a body, mind and spirit just as its bodily host does. And the key to its nature is that with mind, it can speak and reason and take part in existence. Without mind it remains mute. Also, we see that Mind is the fastest thing in the universe; faster than light, it is can traverse the universe in the blink of an eye. This nature is an attribute we find also in the Upanishads, another piece of evidence of the East/West interaction and fusion of knowledge and belief.

Next, we learn about the punishment of the soul and come across the images of the burning fires of hell, so common in Christian images of punishment for the wiccked.

20. Tat. - How then is the human soul punished, father?

H. - What greater punishment is there for the human soul than impiety? What fire makes greater flames than impiety? What savage beast mutilates the body as impiety mutilates the soul? Do you not see how many evils the ungodly soul suffers? How it calls for help and shrieks: 'I am on fire; I am ablaze. I don't know what to say or what to do. Wretch that I am, I am being consumed by the evils which possess me. I cannot see; I cannot hear!' Are they not the voices of a soul which is being punished? Or do you believe, as most do, my son, that the soul at the moment it leaves the body enters that of a beast? This is a very great error.

21. For the soul is punished in the following way. When Nous becomes a divine power, it is obliged to receive a fiery body to serve God; and it enters the impious soul and tortures it with the torments belonging to those that err. Afflicted by these the impious soul turns to murder, outrage and blasphemy and every kind of violence by which men affront justice. But when Nous enters the pious soul it leads it to the light of knowledge. Such a soul is never insolent through sleep, but blesses all men, setting all things right in word and deed, since it is the image of its Father.

Finally in this book we receive the account of the community of the blessed, the role of the father for his children, images taken out into the entire cosmic realm is poetic celebration.

22. Wherefore my son, when giving thanks to God, you should pray for a mind that is noble. Then the soul can pass to a better state, not to a worse. There is a communion of souls and those of the gods communicate with those of men, those of men with creatures. The stronger take care of the weaker, gods of men and men of creatures and God of all; for He is stronger than all; and all are weaker than Him. Thus the cosmos is subject to God, man to the cosmos and the creatures to man. God is above all and around all. The powers of God are like rays, as are the natural powers of the cosmos, and the arts and sciences of men. The powers act throughout the cosmos and upon man through the rays of its nature; the powers of nature act through the elements and men through arts and sciences.

23. This is the governance of the all, depending on the nature of the One, governing through the Nous of the One. Nothing is more divine or effective or more able to unite men to the gods and the gods to men than this Nous. This is the spirit of the Supreme

Good. Blessed is the soul which is wholly filled with it, wretched is the sold which is devoid of it.

In Book 11 we receive a universal vision of the nature of eternity. This imagery reflects one of the central principles of the Hermetic tradition: As above, so below. If the human being has body, mind and soul and spirit, so too does eternity, within which is the cosmos.

The Corpus Hermeticum: Book 11, in which Mind speaks to Hermes
Hermes. - What is the wisdom of God?
Mind. - The Supreme Good, beauty, bliss, every excellence and etemity. As eternity instills immortality and permanence into natter, it orders the cosmos. For the generation of matter depends on eternity, just as eternity depends on God. Generation and time are both in heaven and earth and have two forms: in heaven they are unchangeable and incorruptible; on earth they are both changeable and corruptible. God is the soul of eternity; eternity of the cosmos; and heaven of Earth. God is in Mind, Mind in the soul, soul in matter; and all these things exist through eternity. From within the soul fills this whole body, which contains all bodies, itself being filled by Mind and by God. From without, it contains and enlivens the whole, encompassing this vast and perfect being, the cosmos, and enlivening all creatures from within. Above, in heaven, the identity of the soul remains unchanging, but on earth it gives birth to changing forms.

What we hear and see here is as perfect a description of unity that we shall find in a philosophical text. Above is eternity encompassing the cosmos with God at its head and center within Mind, with Mind in Soul and Soul in matter, existing in Eternity. If human beings are able to find their place in this hierarchy, there can be no separation or isolation, much less loneliness. So when, for example, one of our great physicists declares that the more he understands the universe, the more meaningless it is to him, we can suggest a sermon from Mind as a cure.

In the next chapter, we travel centuries from Alexandria to Florence, Italy, where Cosimo de Medici held sway and studied Plato until one day something remarkable happened.

CHAPTER 8

Ficino and the Soul In Florence

A THOUSAND YEARS after the revelations of the Hermeticists, after the fall of the Roman Empire, after the birth of Islam and the Crusades, after the rise of the monolithic Roman Church and the darkness of the Middle Ages, Cosimo de Medici assumed control of the city of Florence and established a center of learning, of art and culture like no other in Italy.

So determined was he to expand his knowledge and of those around him, that he had agents throughout the Mediterranean bringing him manuscripts to translate and study. In the 1450s his chief translator of Greek was Marcilio Ficino, scholar, physician, teacher, musician, poet, and philosopher. Ficino was working with manuscripts of the dialogues of Plato when one of Cosimo's agents, a monk from Macedonia, arrived one day in 1460 with the manuscripts of the *Corpus Hermeticum*.

The aging Cosimo (he died in 1464) was so intrigued by the promise of the *Corpus* that he told Ficino to stop translating Plato and to work instead on the new manuscripts. If we wonder why his interest was so strongly elevated by his monk's gift, it becomes somewhat clearer when we understand that writings by Hermes Trismegistus were assumed to have been written thousands of years earlier and that the veiled references to Jesus and the Christ must have been revelations and prophesies, thus making Hermes a seer of great power and insight.

So great was Cosimo's and Ficino's mutual respect for Hermes, that Ficino wrote the following tribute to the great philosopher:

Among philosophers [Hermes] first turned from physical and mathematical topics to contemplation of things divine, and he was the first to discuss with great wisdom the majesty of God, the order of demons, and the transformations of souls. Thus, he was called the first author of theology, and Orpheus followed him, taking second place in the ancient theology.... Pythagoras came next in theological succession, having been initiated into the rites of Orpheus, and he was followed by Philolaus, teacher of our divine Plato. In this way, from a wondrous line of six theologians emerged a single system of ancient theology, harmonious in every part.[20]

Although later scholarship revealed the true dating of the Corpus, which would have altered Ficino's estimates of its great importance, we and the rest of interested seekers of wisdom did benefit from the misunderstanding. Without it, the *Corpus* might have simply taken its place on the shelf of other ancient texts, awaiting its turn to contribute to the development of the wisdom traditions of the world, and we would not have had the intense interest and Ficino's subsequent work on the immortality of the soul that we now begin to explore.

In the last chapter we explored the subject matter of the soul, material that Ficino began to translate and Cosimo to read. Later

---

20 *http://plato.stanford.edu/entries/ficino/*

on, after Cosimo's passing, Ficino wrote *Platonic Theology*, Volume I, which contains the following revealing subheadings for Books I-IV: Book I: "Were the soul not immortal, no creature would be more miserable than man"; Book II: "Unity, truth and Goodness are the same thing, and above them there is nothing." Book III: "We descend through the five levels by which we ascended and set up an appropriate comparison between them;" and Book IV: "The are three levels of rational souls: in the first is the world soul, in the second the souls of the spheres, in the third the souls of living creatures contained within the individual spheres." The connection to the Corpus could not be clearer.

It is very nearly enough to reference the subheadings and to move on, but there is much more in Ficino's brilliant text to examine. It is in the character of this polymath and genius that Ficino writes with a forceful optimism, a contrast from the sober Plato, but similar in tone to Hermes. Here is Ficino at the outset of his thesis:

> *Our human minds, "immured in darkness and a sightless dungeon," may look in vain for that light, and we are often driven to doubt our own divine provenance. But I pray that as heavenly souls longing with desire for our heavenly home we may cast off the bonds of our terrestrial chains; cast them off as swiftly as possible, so that, uplifted on Platonic wings and with God as our guide, we may fly unhindered to our ethereal abode, where we will straightway look with joy on the excellence of our own human nature.[21]*

---

21   *Marcilio Ficino, Platonic Theology*, Vol.I, Harvard U. Press, 2001 page 15; hereafter cited as Ficino

Ficino and the Soul In Florence

Before beginning to listen to Ficino, it is useful to describe briefly the grand scheme of reality that he uses to frame his thought. It has a five-part ontological scheme which begins with God, then Angelic Mind, Rational Soul in which we take part, then a level he calls "Quality," which articulates a cohesive force between soul and matter, a level in which human beings may exist and seek to understand and master the other four levels of reality. The level of "quality" is particularly important because it is there, at that central level, where work begins to acquaint ourselves with the soul, to take its measure and to listen to its murmurings. Here is his description of the work to follow in Book I. It is remarkable for its clarity (some credit here to the talents of our translator Michael Allen) and its comprehensive vision.

> *In order to show clearly how best the minds of men can unlock the bars of mortality, witness their own immortality and thus achieve a state of blessedness, I shall try, as best I can, to prove in the following discussion: [first,] that besides this inert mass of our bodies...there exists an active quality or power, to which the Stoics and Cynics direct their investigation; and [second,] that beyond quality, which is divisible along with matter's dimensions and subject to all manner of change, there exists a higher sort of form, which, though it is in a certain sense changeable, admits of no division in a body. In this form the ancient theologians located the seat of the rational soul. This was the point [in the argument] reached by Heraclitus, Marcus Varro and Marcus Manilius. I shall also attempt to show that beyond rational soul exists angelic mind, which is not only indivisible but unchangeable as well. This is the point where Anaxagoras and Hermotimus rested content. But the eye of angelic mind, which seeks for and finds the*

light of truth, is ruled by the divine Sun itself. It is towards this that Plato urges, instructs and enjoins us to direct the gaze of the mind, once it has been purified.

Once we have ascended so far, we shall compare in turn these five levels of being: body (bodily mass), quality, soul, angel and God. Because the genus of rational soul, which occupies the midpoint of these five levels, appears to be the link that holds all nature together — it controls qualities and bodies while it joins itself with angel and with God—I shall demonstrate: [first,] that it is in fact completely indissoluble, because it holds together the different levels of nature; next, that it is preeminent, because it presides over the framework of the world; and finally, that it is most blessed when it steals into the bosom of the divine. I shall seek to establish that the condition and nature of soul is such as I have described, firstly by general arguments, secondly by specific proofs, thirdly by signs, and lastly by resolving questions.[22]

The key to this second paragraph is the importance, call it emphasis, Ficino gives to his level "quality" which, again, he explains as the indissoluble cement holding the whole scheme together. Without 'quality,' in other worlds, we as human beings could not penetrate nor participate in the five levels of being.

If we wonder why Ficino devoted so many pages (about 150) to a discourse on the immortality of the soul and in particular couched in Plato's theological vision, adding his own vision of the five levels, at last one answer is that in Italy at the time, with radical interpretations of the destiny of the human soul in literature and official doctrine, Ficino sought to present a more positive,

---

[22] *Ficino, p.16,17*

less damning view of the soul's journey after death. He also desired of course, to stay clear of heretical involvement at the hands of a paranoid and suspicious Inquisition.

For some clarity on the issue, we can point to the great Divine Comedy of Dante, begun by the poet in 1302 and completed in 1320, a year before his death. The allegory of the *Commedia* takes place beginning on Good Friday and is a parallel account of the Nicene Creed in which Jesus descends into Hell for one day before returning to the world and then ascending to Heaven to sit at the right hand of God. In the poem, the Pilgrim (who is us) finds himself in the dark woods of sin and encounters the figure of Virgil who offers to lead him out of the woods into the light. The journey, however, must pass through Hell, where they navigate circle upon circle or divisions where the damned suffer from sins of indulgence, violence and malice. They encounter Lucifer and passing through his domain (literally over his body) come to Purgatory, where the innocent and ignorant await salvation in limbo.

We can surely assume that Ficino and all the intellectuals of Florence knew Dante's *Commedia* well, and we can see how his Platonic revision would be a central creed of the new Academy. Ficino's life and work endured from the last years of Cosimo de Medici's to the reign of his grandson Lorenzo the Magnificent, who ruled Florence from 1478 to 1492. In those years the new Platonic Academy was founded under Ficino's leadership, and Lorenzo expanded the role of the arts, including in his personal world the likes of Leonardo de Vinci, Botticelli and eventually the young Michelangelo.

For our purposes, though, we will focus attention on the figure of the humanist Pico Della Mirandola, (1463-1494) whose

"Oration on the Dignity of Man" was a remarkable summation of the impulses towards freedom of thought arising from Plato's vision of the examined life and ascent from the confines of the cave of ignorance. Pico's references to the soul is a far cry (literally) from Dante's sin-drenched darkness. Pico wrote:

God the Father, Supreme Architect of the Universe, built this home, this universe we see all around us, a venerable temple of his godhead, through the sublime laws of his ineffable Mind. The expanse above the heavens he decorated with Intelligences, the spheres of heaven with living, eternal souls...Imagine! The great generosity of God! The happiness of man! To man it is allowed to be whatever he chooses to be! As soon as an animal is born, it brings out of its mother's womb all that it will ever possess. Spiritual beings from the beginning become what they are to be for all eternity. Man, when he entered life, the Father gave the seeds of every kind and every way of life possible. Whatever seeds each man sows and cultivates will grow and bear him their proper fruit. If these seeds are vegetative, he will be like a plant. If these seeds are sensitive, he will be like an animal. If these seeds are intellectual, he will be an angel and the son of God. And if, satisfied with no created thing, he removes himself to the center of his own unity, his spiritual soul, united with God, alone in the darkness of God, who is above all things, he will surpass every created thing. Who could not help but admire this great shape-shifter? In fact, how could one admire anything else?

Imagine this declaration set beside the Nicene Creed and how the authorities in Rome reacted to read this oration. At the age of twenty-three Pico proposed 900 theses in which he challenged the powers to debate with him on matters such as the nature of the soul and its destiny. When the proposal finally reached Pope Innocent VIII, the debate was cancelled with this brief condemnation:

> *In part heretical, in part the flower of heresy; several are scandalous and offensive to pious ears; most do nothing but reproduce the errors of pagan philosophers...others are capable of inflaming the impertinence of the Jews; a number of them, finally, under the pretext of 'natural philosophy', favor arts that are enemies to the Catholic faith and to the human race.*

As a result of his challenges and general disturbances of the received traditions of the day, Pico was poisoned and died at the age of 31. His Oration survived on its merits and is still thought to have been one of the finest arguments for the freedom to pursue knowledge for its own sake and to be the clarion call of freedom. It was also in its time a corrective for the nature of the soul in the cosmos and within the human being. Mirandola was an inspiration to any number of thinkers and revolutionaries of the spirit who offended the Church and were tried by the fearsome Inquisition and were imprisoned and burned at the stake

During the extraordinary turbulence of the Italian Renaissance in the 15th Century, it was thinkers like Ficino and Lorenzo and Pico who fomented debate and did the hard work of scholarship and research to give the debate credibility and were able to challenge the errors of doctrine that damaged the Christian faith of its time and prevented Church leadership from even considering the progress being made in science and philosophy.

And it was in the 16th Century that the turbulence of the previous century broke open into violence and revolution. It was science that led the way. In 1512, Copernicus stated that the Earth and the other planets orbited the sun, effectively ending the Earth-centered theory of the universe and with it the human-centered dogmas of the Church. If, the Church reasoned, Earth was not the center of the cosmos, God's position in the cosmos would come under question, and then the whole edifice would crumble.

Then, only five years later, in 1517, Martin Luther posted his 95 theses on the door of the Palast Church in Wittenberg and the Reformation began, and the edifice trembled. As the issues of the Church dogma and practices were being assaulted, the nature of the human soul also rose to the surface in the matter of Christian Mortalism, or the theory known as the "sleep of the soul." The subject arose because Luther advocated the idea that the human soul was not active in the human being but rather slept during its human phase, and only after the death of the body would the soul wake, and then only at Judgment day. In other words, he taught the theory of the dormant soul, or Mortalism.

The Roman Catholic Church had condemned such thinking in the Fifth Council of the Lateran in 1512 as "erroneous assertions." Ironically, it was just before the Reformation that the Church addressed the issue of "sleep of the soul," and it would probably not have emerged as an issue if Luther had not spoken in support of the notion.

Luther's support of Mortalism was followed in the early Reformation by those wishing to challenge Rome, but the notion of the sleeping soul was also accepted by later Protestant denominations as a matter of church authority. If the soul within each human being was active, then the individual could have personal and immediate revelation or access to God. How could the church, then, establish its authority in spiritual matters?

In Eastern traditions, especially Vedanta, the principle of *buddhi*, or perspective choice, refers to self-knowledge attained through the principle of discrimination, or *buddhi*, which is traditionally seen as a function of the mind, but would also be intimately connected to the soul. The Western view of an active soul, as we see in Platonic philosophy, is also the seat of conscience, that sense or feeling within when we stray from moral or ethical behavior.

It would be convenient, then, to maintain the authority of the church to keep the individual soul in the background, or even dormant, to avoid individuals from straying through a personal conviction of insight or revelation. When Emerson, for example, asked in the very first paragraph of *Nature,* "Why should not we have a poetry and philosophy of insight and not of tradition, and a religion by revelation to us, and not the history of theirs?" he was accused of heresy by the leaders of the Unitarian Church, considered by many the most "liberal" of denominations in Christianity. It is, therefore, very possible that the notion of Mortalism, or sleeping soul, would be a convenient dogma to support, that is, if you were a member of the clergy wishing to maintain your authority in doctrinal matters, particularly where revelation is concerned.

Although these references do not specifically name the dormant soul in the living body, nonetheless Luther is referenced by later theologians as supporting the principle. The notion of the sleeping soul was countered by those who teach that when we sleep, the soul, being awake, dreams, travels out of the body returning only when we wake. Arguments took place during this period, not only because Luther mentions the theory of soul sleep, but mostly because of the Reformation itself. As new non-Roman Catholic or Protestant denominations formed, each was free to examine doctrine and formulate its own positions.

In the midst of all this revolutionary activity caused by Luther's reformation movement, the Church in Rome, aided and abetted by the Inquisition, tried to hold its own clergy to the doctrines of the faith and to the authority of the Pope. In its most famous case, that of Giordano Bruno, the attempt failed because of its success, and his story and attitude toward the nature of the soul deserves our attention.

Bruno was a product of the High Renaissance, born in 1548 in Nola, near Naples, well educated, ordained a Dominican friar and was a student of science, astronomy and Platonism. Instinctively, he agreed quickly to the Copernican celestial system, even going beyond it in what was a brilliant intuition to assert that the stars were in fact other suns, many with their own planets where life could also be present. He espoused a Neoplatonic view in cosmology, with unity above as so below from the teaching of Hermes.

After eleven years in the Dominican order, he ran afoul of Rome for asserting the Arian heresy in which Jesus was second to God and not consubstantial or One in nature with the Father. Bruno fled Italy, settling in France where he completed his doctorate in philosophy and began a series of travels resulting from the fame he earned from his teaching.

In 1583 the French King Henry III sent Bruno to England on a political mission, where he became popular for a time in Elizabeth's court. Asked to lecture at Oxford, he again ran afoul of orthodoxy when the tutors there objected to Bruno espousing Neoplatonic theories and controversial scientific views. Fleeing

England, he finally returned to Italy and faced the Inquisition to argue his positions. At his several trials, he defended his ideas and refused to recant them and was finally sentenced to death at the stake, where he was burned to death on 17 February 1600, in the Campo de' Fiori (a central Roman market square), with his "tongue imprisoned because of his wicked words." Each year on this date, rebels and people with causes and contrary beliefs gather and speak to assembled crowds. His large bronze figure, wrapped in a robe with hood, faces Vatican City with a glower.

Theosophy[23] treasures Bruno because he connected the identity of individual souls to the Universal Over-soul. Although he was willing to concede that there were an endless number of individuals, "in the end all are in their nature one, and the knowledge of this unity is the goal of all philosophy." He then proceeded to explain how this knowledge could be acquired:

> *"Within every man," he said, "there is a soul-flame, kindled at the sun of thought, which lends us wings whereby we may approach the sun of knowledge." The soul of man, he affirmed, is the only God there is. "This principle in man moves and governs the body, is superior to the body, and cannot be constrained by it." It is Spirit, the Real Self," in which, from which and through which are formed the different bodies, which have to pass through different kinds of existences, names and destinies."*

So, why is it relevant to our discussion of soul to reference both Luther and Bruno? The answer is that in Luther we had an unhappy and angry priest whose 95 theses attacked the Church for its

---

23 The "theosophy" was first used in writing during the 3rd to the 6th Century CE by the Alexandrian Neo-Platonic philosophers. They used this term to denote an experiential knowledge that came through spiritual, not intellectual, means.

corruption and immoral practices, such as the policy of traveling priests selling "indulgences" to relieve the faithful of their sins as well as their money. His was a reformation of conduct and policy, whereas Bruno was executed because his ideas were dangerous because if his ideas proved to be true or accepted by the people, Rome would lose its authority in the glow of the people's personal freedom to think for themselves. Also, Luther was successful in part because the rulers in Europe saw in the Reformation an opportunity to get from under the heel of Rome, to seize Church lands and to establish Christian countries on their own terms. Those countries like France and Spain that remained Catholic were rewarded, and those like Germany and the northern countries who joined the Reformation were punished but were free and sovereign in ways that France and Spain were not. However, religious wars were fought with impunity. From 1564 through 1580, for example, there were seven religious wars in France alone.

In this climate, esoteric issues like the nature of the soul were not to be seriously revived until the Enlightenment, when philosophy and religion went their separate ways. Church retained its view of the personal soul belonging to one embodiment. The question of soul in philosophy was set aside in favor of the mind/body question. Even the word "soul" gradually disappeared from view. The issue in philosophy wasn't dormancy, but rather the very existence of the soul.

That said, however, there remained through the Enlightenment an esoteric strain of philosophy beholden to Platonic, Neoplatonic, Eastern and Hermetic teachings that came to be called by Leibniz the Perennial Philosophy. It carried a wisdom tradition that found its way through heresies, executions, reformations, doctrines, and even pogroms. Following the Enlightenment of the Eighteenth

Ficino and the Soul In Florence

Century, the Romantics Wordsworth and Coleridge, and then the German Idealists Schelling, Hegel and Kant, took up the thinking in the form of Idealism, and in that form it crossed the Atlantic Ocean to Concord, Massachusetts to the New England Transcendentalists, who opened the doors of inquiry to the nature of soul once again.

In the next chapter, we will examine how one philosopher, Ralph Waldo Emerson, reexamined and reformed the soul to be an organic part of a philosophy of personal self-recovery.

CHAPTER 9

Emerson and the Over- Soul

AT THE CLOSE of the last chapter, mention was made of the Perennial Philosophy, that thread of the Idealist philosophy that appeared first in the East with Advaita Vedanta, the divinely centered philosophy of unity, traveled west into Greece and was articulated most clearly by Plotinus and then was gathered together again by Ficino in his Platonic Academy. As a philosophy Idealism is formally described as:

1. *something mental (the mind, spirit, reason, will) is the ultimate foundation of all reality, or even exhaustive of reality, and*
2. *although the existence of something independent of the mind is conceded, everything that we can know about this mind-independent "reality" is held to be so permeated by the creative, formative, or constructive activities of the mind (of some kind or other) that all claims to knowledge must be considered, in some sense, to be a form of self-knowledge.*[24]

Idealism, then, is centered in the mind, and among its most vehement supporters, Emerson articulated as central to his

---
24 *http://plato.stanford.edu/entries/idealism*

philosophy the existence of Universal Mind, which he terms Intellect. The universal mind is also connected directly to God and the soul, with little doubt or misunderstanding. In *Nature*, Emerson's first published work in 1836, Emerson wrote: "Idealism beholds the whole circle of persons and things...as one vast picture which God paints on the instant eternity for the contemplation of the soul." In Emerson the soul is reborn.

And then, in subsequent work over a lifetime of writing and publication, he made reference to the soul over 650 times. The task here, then, will be to select and connect those references to the thread of the Perennial Philosophy and to the key moments in the journey of the soul to Emerson's doorstep and beyond.

That the soul in Emerson's work is awake in the individual, present in the cosmos, and central to the life of the mind, is without debate. His references may in some cases suggest a "feeling center" in human character, but for the most part, the soul is a living entity which consorts with mind to illuminate reality and truth.

What follows are several references to the soul in *Nature*, the small book of only ninety pages where Emerson sets forth his interpretation of Idealism and which began in the New England the movement to be known as Transcendentalism. Here are a series of key statements, grouped in order to fix the principle in mind:

Man is conscious of a universal soul within or behind his individual life...
This universal soul [man] calls Reason...
...every object rightly seen, unlocks a new faculty of the soul and... what difference does it make, whether Orion is up there

in heaven, or some god paints the image in the firmament of the soul?

It is, in both cases [Plato and Sophocles]...that this feeble human being has penetrated the vast masses of nature with an informing soul...

...we think of nature as an appendix to the soul.

...[external beauty] is the frail and weary weed, in which God dresses the soul which he has called into time.

Let [the ideal theory] stand then...merely as a useful introductory hypothesis, serving to apprize us of the eternal distinction between the soul and the world.

We learn that the highest is present to the soul of man;...

The problem of restoring to the world original and eternal beauty is solved by the redemption of the soul.

Is not prayer also...a sally of the soul into the unfound infinite?

And finally, "This [spiritual] view...animates me to create my own world through the purification of my soul." This last reference from *Nature* leads us now into the body of Emerson's work and the role that the soul plays in creating our own world through the presence and work of the soul within.

This last quote from *Nature* may suggest in his use of the word "purification" a religious theme of a repentance from sin, but if we look at the whole quote we see that purification relates to creating "my own world.." It is, then, a purification from the external influences, from society's directions, the desires of others, the teacher's instructions, the church's doctrines and so on that need to be purified from our soul before we can become purely self-reliant.

Most people who know something about Emerson know that he is famous for his most well-known essay "Self-Reliance." A careful reading of that great essay shows that Emerson's intent in that plea for independence of thought and action in life is really about self-recovery, or a purification of thought and action from external influence and a determined effort to live life from within, not in isolation but in full engagement in the world. If we look at the use of the references to the soul in "Self-Reliance" we can make that connection more clearly.

The essay begins with an admonition in Latin: "Ne te quaesiveris extra" or "Do not look for yourself outside." It is inside where we find ourselves, and the soul is where the core of our nature (or reality) resides. The essay begins very strangely, and its import is often missed.

"I read the other day some verses written by an eminent painter which were original and not conventional." Poetry written by a painter? That does suggest originality and unconventional all right. Emerson's point is to turn our attention away from the ordinary and expected. Here is our author reading verses composed by a painter. What painter and what verses matters little. The next sentence is the important message: "The soul always hears an admonition in such lines, let the subject be what it may."

What admonition does the soul hear? Originality and the unconventional. As he says later on, "Imitation is suicide." The self is lost in imitation, and it is the soul that hears, and our task is to listen to the soul's urging for the original. Further on he gives us one of his most famous admonitions:

A foolish consistency is the hobgoblin of little minds, adored by little statesmen and philosophers and divines. With consistency a great soul has simply nothing to do. He may as well concern himself with his shadow on the wall. Speak what you think now in hard words, and to-morrow speak what to-morrow thinks in hard words again, though it contradict every thing you said to-day. — 'Ah, so you shall be sure to be misunderstood.' — Is it so bad, then, to be misunderstood? Pythagoras was misunderstood, and Socrates, and Jesus, and Luther, and Copernicus, and Galileo, and Newton, and every pure and wise spirit that ever took flesh. To be great is to be misunderstood.

It is fortuitous that in the last portion of that paragraph are the names of historical figures referenced in the exploration of soul throughout history, examples of independence and certainly misunderstood figures as well. But for our purposes, it is the great soul that has nothing to do with consistency, not steadfastness but rather unwinding and unraveling the habits of thought and action. As Emerson says, is it is a foolish consistency that the great soul abhors.

Further along he explains to us what he means by foolish consistency and once again, the soul is the judge:

We denote this primary wisdom as Intuition, whilst all later teachings are tuitions. In that deep force, the last fact behind which analysis cannot go, all things find their common origin. For, the sense of being which in calm hours rises, we know not how, in the soul, is not diverse from things, from space, from light, from time, from man, but one with them, and proceeds obviously from the same source whence their life and being also proceed.

Here we find Emerson's pleas for calm hours in which the soul can be felt in our sense of being. His capitalization of Intuition here denotes the universal source of knowledge. It is not a tuition, meaning an external instruction, but inner in-tuition which rises from we know not where but still can be trusted. As he says: "We lie in the lap of immense intelligence, which makes us receivers of its truth and organs of its activity. When we discern justice, when we discern truth, we do nothing of ourselves, but allow a passage to its beams. If we ask whence this comes, if we seek to pry into the soul that causes, all philosophy is at fault."

At one point in the essay Emerson addresses the question of the truth and values of these intuitions, of how we can trust these insights: Here is his reply:

I remember an answer which when quite young I was prompted to make to a valued adviser, who was wont to importune me with the dear old doctrines of the church. On my saying, What have I to do with the sacredness of traditions, if I live wholly from within? my friend suggested, — "But these impulses may be from below, not from above." I replied, "They do not seem to me to be such; but if I am the Devil's child, I will live then from the Devil." No law can be sacred to me but that of my nature.

The key to that defense is the line "They do not seem to me to be..." which is the point. Without that sentence his claim might be madness, but his powers of intuitive discrimination saves him from false testimony. As one famous critic once said about Emerson: "The annoying thing about him is that he's always right!" In other words, the more we examine and question, the more his thought holds up. We can deny his Idealism, but not his insights within it.

To go back then, to the matter if "prying" into the soul, what exactly does it mean to pry into the soul? It is a failure of trust. What does it mean to pry? It is an intrusion into another's privacy, an unwelcome and uninvited failure of trust. Therefore, prying into the intuitions of the soul is such an intrusion, a low curiosity and a meanness of spirit. Self-trust is the aim, and that begins with accepting the intuitions of the soul as valid, in fact, sacred. As he says, again, " The relations of the soul to the divine spirit are so pure, that it is profane to seek to interpose helps." What are helps? They are external methods, directions, systems, shortcuts, ruminations, considerings, rationalizations of all kinds. We harbor these thoughts and seek out these so-called helps so much that we ruin our days with them. If you have an impulse you think might come from the soul, but doesn't, the wakened soul will turn your stomach in protest. As Socrates put it, "When I consider doing some wrong, my soul rises up and says, "No!"

When Emerson asked in his introduction to *Nature*, "Why can we not have a revelation to us and not a history of theirs?" he was speaking of our weak dependence on historical revelation and doctrines to tell us what to do and think instead of listening in the silence of reflection to what the soul tells us. In "Self-Reliance" Emerson does not stand still and neither does the soul. We enter in mid-essay into new territory which takes us away from complacency and a static certainty. We are told not to stand still:

> *Life only avails, not the having lived. Power ceases in the instant of repose; it resides in the moment of transition from a past to a new state, in the shooting of the gulf, in the darting to an aim. This one fact the world hates, that the soul becomes; for that for ever degrades the past, turns all riches to poverty, all reputation*

to a shame, confounds the saint with the rogue, shoves Jesus and Judas equally aside. Why, then, do we prate of self-reliance? Inasmuch as the soul is present, there will be power not confident but agent.

The soul understood in its verb form, 'to agent' is an active power, and as a noun like 'an agent,' it finds us work, calls us up and gets us off the couch, tells us we have an audition, a job, a risk to take, a song to sing, work to deliver. Therefore, he says, "The genesis and maturation of a planet, its poise and orbit, the bended tree recovering itself from the strong wind, the vital resources of every animal and vegetable, are demonstrations of the self-sufficing, and therefore self-relying soul."

And it is that this active power means that we have to get up and go somewhere, travel in order to improve the mind, experience new things, Emerson clarifies his centering principles of self-containment offer instruction:

The soul is no traveller; the wise man stays at home, and when his necessities, his duties, on any occasion call him from his house, or into foreign lands, he is at home still, and shall make men sensible by the expression of his countenance, that he goes the missionary of wisdom and virtue, and visits cities and men like a sovereign, and not like an interloper or a valet.

Emerson knew exactly what he was talking about because for most of his working life, he was on the road for six months of every year lecturing, and crossing the Atlantic by sail and steam to England, Europe, even Egypt, but he was always at home within himself, his soul not concerned with Tuesday, London, or Boston,

The Soul's Journey

the season or the year, and that stillness within was crucial and was noted by his audiences, who saw before them a man who was centered, unruffled, and steady on his course.

On one occasion, lecturing in Boston, a reporter stood in the rear trying to take notes to report for the morning paper, but he couldn't grasp the meaning. Standing next to him was a maid with a broom, waiting to sweep that hall and close up for the night. The reporter turned to her and asked, "Do you know what he's talking about?" The maid replied, "No, but I see and hear the man and I know he's telling me the truth." That certainty of appearance and sound is the authority of the soul. He put the matter himself this way:

> *There is at this moment for you an utterance brave and grand as that of the colossal chisel of Phidias, or trowel of the Egyptians, or the pen of Moses, or Dante, but different from all these. Not possibly will the soul all rich, all eloquent, with thousand-cloven tongue, deign to repeat itself; but if you can hear what these patriarchs say, surely you can reply to them in the same pitch of voice; for the ear and the tongue are two organs of one nature.*

Once centered in the soul, like the student Tat to Hermes, we have the power to talk to anyone as long as we hold still enough to listen to the authority within. The reference to a thousand-cloven tongue in the soul expands its reach and nature. Emerson taught that the soul was both personal and universal, a principle we have seen before, but in his treatment and expression the range and nature take on a rich habitation.

We pass now to the central examination of the nature of the soul in the essay "The Over-Soul," where over sixty references to the soul, basically the entire essay, deals with Emerson's knowledge of the soul in the broadest and most eloquent expression of its range and power.

In its broadest sense, he says, " The philosophy of six thousand years has not searched the chambers and magazines of the soul." So we are warned to prepare to be astounded as well as refreshed.

As to eloquence, a quality for which Emerson was famous, very few passages exceed in that quality than the second paragraph of "The Over-Soul." It deserves to be read and heard in its entirety:

The Supreme Critic on the errors of the past and the present, and the only prophet of that which must be, is that great nature in which we rest, as the earth lies in the soft arms of the atmosphere; that Unity, that Over-soul, within which every man's particular being is contained and made one with all other; that common heart, of which all sincere conversation is the worship, to which all right action is submission; that overpowering reality which confutes our tricks and talents, and constrains every one to pass for what he is, and to speak from his character, and not from his tongue, and which evermore tends to pass into our thought and hand, and become wisdom, and virtue, and power, and beauty. We live in succession, in division, in parts, in particles. Meantime within man is the soul of the whole; the wise silence; the universal beauty, to which every part and particle is equally related; the eternal ONE. And this deep power in which we exist, and whose beatitude is all accessible to us, is not only self-sufficing and perfect in every hour, but the act of seeing and the thing seen, the seer and the spectacle, the subject and the object, are one. We see the world piece by piece, as the sun, the moon, the animal, the tree; but the whole, of which these are the shining parts, is the soul. Only by the vision of that Wisdom can the horoscope of the ages be read, and by falling back on our better thoughts, by yielding to the spirit of prophecy which is innate in every man, we can know what it saith. Every man's words, who speaks from that life, must sound vain to those who do not dwell in the same thought on their own part. I dare not speak for it. My words do not carry its august sense; they fall short and cold. Only itself can inspire whom it will, and behold! their speech shall be lyrical, and sweet, and universal as the rising of the wind. Yet I desire, even by profane words, if I may not use sacred, to indicate the heaven of this deity, and to report what hints I have collected of the transcendent simplicity and energy of the Highest Law.

It is Emerson's gift to us that we have this portrait of the soul. It cannot have been easy to paint, so universal, cosmic and yet interior, invisible and silent is its nature. Nonetheless I know of no other text with as complete a description in relatively few words. Ficino's book on the soul, in approximately 150 pages is very nearly opaque in comparison, and tracts from the German Idealists are too erudite and convoluted for our edification, much less inspiration. But here, on the other hand, we have what can only be described as a fireworks of expression illuminating the blackness of the night sky.

Critics have always complained that Emerson's prose is such that we can never tell where a famous quotation comes from. It's as if, they say, he really wrote one great work, randomly divided into chapters, which is why it is thought he wrote only one book, and it was twelve volumes long. But in "The Over-Soul" those seekers after Being and the life and nature of soul have their compact text to study and master. Our more limited task will be only to highlight the main principles in order to guide the viewer standing before the portrait, suggesting as we move on in the Emerson gallery that as an individual we might return on a day when the gallery is nearly empty, just us, the guard, and perhaps a student sketching a copy, so that you can study in peace and quiet.

Here, then, are some images, at the very center of the picture, to contemplate.

> *All goes to show that the soul in man is not an organ, but animates and exercises all the organs; is not a function, like the power of memory, of calculation, of comparison, but uses these as hands and feet; is not a faculty, but a light; is not the intellect or the will, but the master of the intellect and the will; is the background of our being, in which they lie, — an immensity not possessed and that cannot be possessed.*

This approach is what we call an apophatic definition, saying through the negative what the soul is not: — not a function, not a power of mind, not a faculty, not the intellect or will, and not to be possessed. These are vital negatives, leaving us with the positives: a light, a guide, a background and an immensity. This description clearly frames a universal entity which we share and have access to. Therefore, we learn that "The soul looketh steadily forwards, creating a world before her, leaving worlds behind her. She has no dates, nor rites, nor persons, nor specialties, nor men. The soul knows only the soul; the web of events is the flowing robe in which she is clothed."

Is there then, wrapped in this definition, an individual soul, an entity that is ours alone, a something that continues, perhaps to embody again as in reincarnation? That is the question, saith Hamlet, the introspective prince. It is an answer devoutly to be answered. Emerson is an honest man, however, and does not speculate. Here is his estimate of these questions we all ask:

> *Men ask concerning the immortality of the soul, the employments of heaven, the state of the sinner, and so forth. They even dream that Jesus has left replies to precisely these interrogatories. Never a moment did that sublime spirit speak in their patois [accent]. To truth, justice, love, the attributes of the soul, the idea of immutableness is essentially associated. Jesus, living in these moral sentiments, heedless of sensual fortunes, heeding only the manifestations of these, never made the separation of the idea of duration from the essence of these attributes, nor uttered a syllable concerning the duration of the soul. It was left to his disciples to sever duration from the moral elements, and to teach the immortality of the soul as a doctrine, and maintain it by evidences. The moment the doctrine of the immortality is separately taught, man is already fallen. In the flowing of love, in the adoration of humility, there is no question of continuance. No inspired man ever asks this question, or condescends to these evidences. For the soul is true to itself, and the man in whom it is shed abroad cannot wander from the present, which is infinite, to a future which would be finite.*

> *These questions which we lust to ask about the future are a confession of sin. God has no answer for them. No answer in words can reply to a question of things. It is not in an arbitrary "decree of God," but in the nature of man, that a veil shuts down on the facts of to-morrow; for the soul will not have us read any other*

cipher than that of cause and effect. By this veil, which curtains events, it instructs the children of men to live in to-day. The only mode of obtaining an answer to these questions of the senses is to forego all low curiosity, and, accepting the tide of being which floats us into the secret of nature, work and live, work and live, and all unawares the advancing soul has built and forged for itself a new condition, and the question and the answer are one.

Emerson's maturity shines through here, but also is his devotion to us, and his answer to our curiosity is the correct one. He adds this note, which in the light of our exploration to date, should be a reminder: "The faith that stands on authority is not faith. The reliance on authority measures the decline of religion, the withdrawal of the soul." We shall in our final chapter see what happens when the soul withdraws and is replaced by a variety of self-proclaimed authorities and why it is critical to take our own temperature in this fevered anxiety of knowing.

We leave the last word to Emerson as he closes this essay on the nature of the soul.

Thus revering the soul, and learning, as the ancient said, that "its beauty is immense," man will come to see that the world is the perennial miracle which the soul worketh, and be less astonished at particular wonders; he will learn that there is no profane history; that all history is sacred; that the universe is represented in an atom, in a moment of time. He will weave no longer a spotted life of shreds and patches, but he will live with a divine unity. He will cease from what is base and frivolous in his life, and be content with all places and with any service he can render.

The Soul's Journey

He will calmly front the morrow in the negligency of that trust which carries God with it, and so hath already the whole future in the bottom of the heart.

CHAPTER 10

Consciousness and Soul in our Time

Closing our discussion of Emerson's vision and experience with the Over-Soul, we move on to the Twentieth Century and into the present. If we are given the task of assigning to one individual the title of most important life and work in the Twentieth Century, the title goes to Albert Einstein. It is not just his insight into the relationship of matter and energy in the birth of atomic power, but it is also the resulting development from his theories of quantum mechanics in what has become the single most important technological development in human history.

His work meant that in the universe matter than tells space how to bend and space tells matter how to move. It meant that time was now another dimension, and we invented space/time. It meant that matter did not need to have a local force to move it, but non-locality suggested that matter could be moved instantaneously, faster than the speed of light, moved by a signal light-years distant. It meant that particles could be waves and waves particles and that we could not calculate the position of a particle and its momentum at the same time. Wonder piled on to wonders.

Consider the state of science and religion at the close of the Nineteenth Century: two disciplines who could not, would not, talk to one another. Science was hardened into the material world, and religion was dependent on myths of spirit and articles of faith. But when the import of the atomic age and the evolution of quantum mechanics met a new and invigorated spiritual revolution, led by Eastern teachers and gurus, matter and spirit began to communicate, and the result was an invigoration of spiritual knowledge and understanding.

It wasn't just the fact that three satellites in space could tell us how to get to Grandmother's house, or that walking down the street we could talk to a friend in Moscow. These were the daily miracles of the quantum universe. What was also emerging was the realization that these miracles could also translate to a new understanding of the universe itself. As human beings, we were not longer strangers in the strange place. We had begun to merge with the cosmos. The Hubble telescope showed us images of the universe at its inception. We watched galaxies merging ten billion light-years away, and also learned that in this moment in time those galaxies were gone, out of sight because the universe was expanding at an increasing rate.

We also learned the universe contained only a small percentage of visible matter, less than ten percent and that most of the universe was made up of dark or invisible matter and energy. And perhaps the most astonishing was the admission of normally staid scientists that the universe might well be infinite, a word normally the property of theologians. And further, some cosmologists began to suspect that space/time might well be an illusion, that we ourselves were illusory as well. Such speculation drew us back to Eastern philosophy and the concept of Maya, or illusory existence, leaving us afloat, our feet no longer touching the illusory ground.

Consciousness and Soul in our Time

As it happened, the major theme of the later Twentieth Century turned out to be a multi-disciplinary exploration from the ground up into the nature of consciousness. The ground in this case was brain research and the search for sources of consciousness and the nature of mind. After thousands of books and papers, the mystery remains.

Further up the chain of being came the search through ancient sources, like the Upanishads, translations of which became available for study and in some cases illuminating. Like the materials in previous chapters from Eastern, Greek, and Hermetic texts, consciousness extended past the brain into nature and into the cosmos. We began to speculate that, perhaps, the nature and function of consciousness was not in us but rather we were in it. This insight would not have arisen as clearly as it did had it not been for the developments in what we now call the New Physics – relativity and the quantum world.

Then, as we watched the same changes in religion, where the soul holds sway over lives and immortality, study also flourished as if permission had been granted to open the door to secret rooms where soul studies were gathering dust. In this case science did not enter these rooms, but philosophers and theologians sat quietly, reading and writing new books and papers. Could the nature of the soul correspond in the same way to the ideas about a cosmic consciousness? Could the soul, too, be pervasive, in which case it is not in us but we are in it?

A consciousness of soul, as it turns out, is universal among the peoples of the world. Throughout, the traditional way for people to greet one another contains a recognition of the existence of an immortal soul and human identity with one another. Here are examples: In India we say Namaste, meaning "The divinity in me recognizes and honors the divinity in you;" in Mayan, "In-Lakesh," "I am another you;" in Africa, "Eh-ti-zain," How is your soul perceiving the world?" in Lakota (native American), "Mitakuye Oaysin, "All are related;" In Polynesia, "Aloha," "I recognize the presence of divine breath in you;" In German, "Gruss Got," "Greetings, God in you."

These forms of greeting are meant to transcend surface appearances encountered in greeting and intend to make a connection at a spiritual level. Consider what takes place in consciousness when we are asked "How is your soul perceiving the world?" Even if the greeting is somewhat mechanical in everyday relations, its deeper meaning penetrates the sub-conscious to establish a deeper connection.

Thus, when the word "Namaste" is spoken, with palms together and a slight bow, the soul is elevated into the moment between those present. It is an acknowledgment of that reality, not as a religious observance but more naturally as a connection to nature and life itself at its most complete and sacred.

This sense of mutual identity and commonality among people has – it will surprise no one to know – been lost to us. We can trace this process through a few examples. In the Sixties, a time when we read books like "Coming Apart," and our culture was noticeably in crisis, two developments illustrated the extent of that crisis. First, books like Sypher's *Loss of the Self in Modern Literature and Art* (1962), described the fragmentation of the self and catalogued the featureless man and the absence of a recognizable human being in a mechanical world. At the same time the psychologist Erik Erikson at Harvard began seeing students at the Health Service who were, in his words, having a crisis of identity. They didn't know who they were, they said, or what they were meant to do. The phenomenon was recognized among many college campuses and eventually appeared at the high school level as well. It was a virus of the spirit.

Twenty years later, in 1986, just as the computer age was being born and the Internet was beginning to connect people all over the world, the philosopher William Barrett wrote a book entitled *The Death of the Soul*. In it, he talked about what he called the phenomenon of "dispersion," a fragmentation of the self in which individuals began to lose the notion of a coherent identity.

Barrett equated the self with the soul in his argument, suggesting that increasingly he had no sense of "I" as an identity, but that he felt fragmented and separated from himself, meaning that he had lost control of an integrated self as part of the world and beyond that of the cosmos. This separation created a lonely, distracted sense of presence and a severe loneliness, even when surrounded by family, friends and colleagues.

Then, twenty year after that, in 2006, the smart phone arrived and with it the focus of the 'selfie,' a symptom of a severe fragmentation and an almost frantic obsession to retrieve the self from the abyss. Staring at our own image and focusing attention for hours and hours on whatever pops up on the little screen, is a symptom of radical dispersion and the attempted recovery of the diminished self.

We are referred to now as device people, hooked to machines that give us the impression that we are once again whole, not fragments or dispersed. And yet the effect is counter-productive, because the device is not who or what we are. Unlike the television or computer, these devices are conveniently portable. A recent article in the *New York Review of Books* tells us that three quarters of eighteen-to-twenty-year olds reach for their phones as soon as they wake up, and they check their phones 200 or more times a day, on average every four minutes. We don't walk down the street looking around any more, focused instead on the little screen. And perhaps what is more telling is that we don't use the phone to talk, but instead to text, it being even less personal.

There is, of course, a segment of society that, seeing all this, has reacted and taken steps to either reverse this crisis or else remain above it altogether. A new focus on the nature of consciousness has produced thousands of books in the past two decades trying to describe and define the source and nature of conscious experience. What is revealing, however, is the lack of consensus among philosophers and scientists and medical researchers as to what exactly consciousness is, and as a result the theories abound and become more and more radical and less helpful to those of us seeking knowledge and understanding.

As to the soul, there is silence. What we have seen in our journey down through history tells us not to be surprised by this silence. The only exception has been in the New Age movement. James Hillman's *The Soul's Code*, for example, does not seek to define the soul, but to use the term as synonymous with the self in the Jungian sense. Thomas Moore's *Care of the Soul* was an exception in giving the soul an identity separate from self and exploring ways to live within a sacred setting or context in which we can create a more spiritual life.

But there is much more to say about the soul that we have described in the powerful figures central to our study, that is the Indic authors, and Plato, Plotinus, Ficino, Bruno, and Emerson. But the most important influences for our own time and further study, were first, Pythagoras and then the mythical Hermes and the Hermetic writers. Let's see why that is the case.

Rather than including a full discussion of the Discourse of the Eight and Ninth Gates of initiation in the Hermetic material, I have saved a fuller discussion of it for last because this important Hermetic and Gnostic text was discovered in 1946, contained in the Nag Hammadi documents. Its content is different from the other texts because Hermes is the teacher and the goal of the teaching is the initiation into the realm of Universal Mind. Because of its late discovery, the discourse of Hermes as it is now known belongs to us and not to the past.

In the Nag Hammadi text, the discourse has a special introduction from Douglas Parrrott, the beginning of which follows:

Although its title is lost, this tractate has been identified as Hermetic from the use of the names Trismegistus and Hermes and close similarities with previously known Hermetic tractates. It has been named from its contents, using a phrase found in the tractate itself. It describes in dialogue form the process by which a spiritual guide (mystagogue) leads an initiate to a mystical experience.

The eighth and the ninth indicate the eighth and ninth spheres surrounding the earth. In ancient times it was thought that the first seven spheres were the realms of the sun, moon, and planets, the lower powers whose control over human life was not necessarily benevolent. The eighth and ninth spheres thus designate the beginning of the divine realm, the levels beyond the control of the lower powers. At death the soul would journey through the seven spheres, and after successful passage it would reach the eighth and the ninth, the levels at which the soul could experience true bliss. Furthermore, the eighth and the ninth spheres can also indicate advanced stages of spiritual development. The tractate possibly

The Soul's Journey

assumes yet another sphere, a higher, tenth sphere, where God himself dwells, though this is not entirely clear.

The imagery and context in which the soul develops and seeks its eventual destination are expressed in principles of astronomy, astrology and even the musical scale, the pattern for which we celebrate Pythagoras. Musically, when we ascend the octave, we experience whole tones (in the key of C) from the initial C to D to E, but then from E to F we encounter a half tone. In some spiritual traditions involving progress of development in insight, that step is thought to need a special impulse, a help from a teacher to reach the fourth step or tone in the scale. Then, from that fourth step, which brings with it a clearer knowledge of the next levels, level five, or G leads naturally to A, but then in order to reach level seven, or B, another awkward moment, a half tone requires initiation again, a step in which the initiate perceives the divine order but has yet to reach or join with it.

As we see in the explanation above that level eight or Eighth Gate is the first level of the divine realm, where the Nous or Universal Mind dwells. The seventh position, just before the octave is the highest state or gate that human beings normally reach in their spiritual growth. Our student, however, in this discourse desires to reach the octave, a new higher key earned through study, grace, and special initiation.

He asks his teacher what he must do to reach this stage of development and the answer comes first from prayer:

Lord, grant us a wisdom from your power that reaches us, so that we may describe to ourselves the vision of the eighth and the ninth. We have already advanced to the seventh, since we are pious and walk in your law. And your will we fulfill always. For we have walked in your way, so that your vision may come. Lord, grant us the truth in the image. Allow us through the spirit to see the form of the image that has no deficiency, and receive the reflection of the abundance from us through our praise. And acknowledge the spirit that is in us. For from you the universe received soul.

Through the teaching the student receives the light and then in turn becomes a teacher because he "sees" the image of the Universal Mind and dwells within its power. In the spiritual work of various schools, including Theosophical study, schools of Vedanta, Jnana Yoga and others, these images of gates, circles of knowledge, and scales of advancement, initiations of various kinds are created to mark progress as well as levels of understanding.

Empirically, we can establish levels or planes of thought through psychological and physiological measurement as well as by intellectual evaluation of a person's development and progress.[25] The various stages we progress through can be described as Sexual (plane2), Intention (Plane 3), Emotion (Plane 4), Intellect (Plane 5) and Spirit (Plane 7). The jump from five to seven signifies the great leap from the mental plane to the spiritual, a step which we see in the Hermetic material and which requires instruction and initiation.

This framing of planes or stages in development fits comfortably within the octave structure as well. The addition of gates or planes eight and nine are not human but rather transcendental or divine. As we see in the prayer prior to the initiation (the ritual of

---

25 C. Robert Cloninger, *Feeling Good, the Science of Well-Being*, Oxford, 2004

which is not recorded in the discourse – or it was excised from it) we have a reference of the soul, received from God to the universe.

As we saw in Emerson, his comprehensive study of soul concentrates on its universal nature, with the tacit implication that we participate in this presence. What fate or destiny this implies remains uncertain, as it should be. And yet, the implications we have from our study give us important clues provided by the wisdom of those who have passed through gates or planes of study and knowledge.

In the discourse, after the initiation, Hermes instructs the youth to include an oath in the book of knowledge and truth that he is required to deposit in the sanctuary, and the instruction is important to our concerns. Hermes says:

> *"Write an oath in the book, lest those who read the book bring the language into abuse, and not (use it) to oppose the acts of fate. Rather, they should submit to the law of God, without having transgressed at all, but in purity asking God for wisdom and knowledge. And he who will not be begotten at the start by God and comes to be by the general and guiding discourses, will not be able to read the things written in this book, even though his conscience is pure within him, or not doing anything shameful, nor does he consent to it. Rather, by stages he must advance and enter into the way of immortality. And thus he enters into the understanding of the eighth that reveals the ninth."*

This requirement that immortality is earned through stages and study was central to the Hermetic tradition, which means that the Hermitic discipline was strict and ascent difficult. If, then, we look at the stages of human thought leading to spiritual knowledge, we encounter stages of personal development we can easily recognize in ourselves.

For example, plane 3, Intention, might be unfamiliar in terminology but consider the stages within that plane. In the sexual stage of intention (2), the characteristics are aimless desire and fighting. In the material stage (3), the characteristics are greed and competition. In the emotional stage (4), the qualities are anger, envy or stoicism. In the intellectual stage (5) we find pride or inferiority. And in the spiritual stage (7) the characteristics are desire for power or expression of sarcasm.

When we reach Plane 7 and look back at the positive attributes in its progress, we find that in our humanity of sexual, intentional, emotional and mental lives there are positive qualities. We see, for example, in the Emotional sub-plane that the positive characteristic is self-acceptance and contentment. In the Intellect plane (5) the spiritual characteristics are self-actualization and a sense of universal participation. And in plane 7 of Spirit, the spiritual aspect is primarily coherence or unity. The seeker here experiences Oneness. Separation has disappeared, We are whole. We can see, then, what Hermes means by speaking about the need for the seeker to move through the proper stages of development with guidance, so that the lower stages of development can be recognized and corrected in order to be positive.

Just as an example, if a spiritual teacher has a group of students seeking spiritual guidance and one of them is still in the Intention stage 3 of thought, he will exhibit a greedy approach to acquiring knowledge and be competitive towards the other students. Therefore, it is important that those who seek the highest levels of self-actualization must be at level 7 in Intellect before they leap to the Spiritual level 7.

For another example, if a person is heard to say, "I'm at a very high stage of spiritual development," a listener at a lower stage might say, "Wow that's great, what's it like?" whereas a person who is in fact at a higher stage of development might say, "How about a cup of tea, over there on the bench by the waterfall." As the water cascades and the tea is calming, a meaningful conversation might take place.

Another kind of spiritual development, also involving the number seven, are the seven attainments of a life of accomplishment. In ancient times the seven were called the Trivium and Quadrivium or seven subjects of Liberal Arts. In a more contemporary educational setting these might be Mathematics, Astronomy, Biology and Physics, Social and Political Science, Music and Art, Language, and Philosophy. The soul is essential in these attainments in that what we attain in these seven areas of knowledge is a consciousness which feeds the soul and enhances spiritual strength. And as to reincarnation, it seems that it would take many lifetimes to master the seven stages of development as well as the seven attainments of life on this planet, much less prepare for stages eight and nine, what ever they might be.

As a last look at soul in a spiritual life, we can recall the wisdom traditions from East and West that invariably retain the presence of a divine force called soul, which along with a universal mind, permeates the cosmos and gives it substance. And because we are part of that cosmic whole and not separated from it because we sometimes feel its vastness and silence, but are in fact one with it always, we can fall still at times and enter that vastness and feel and know we are welcome and will probably stay, even after this body we care for will return to the elements that made it so as to make another one.

And what is crucial within those final moments of our final falling still, it is the accomplished soul that, knowing its place and destiny because we were conscious partners, will move on, perhaps carrying a piece of our consciousness on its journey as a well deserved token of gratitude. As Prince Hamlet expressed it, "Tis a consummation devoutly to be wished."

Printed in Great Britain
by Amazon